Robert Louis Stevenson (13 November 1850 – 3 December 1894) was a Scottish novelist and travel writer, most noted for Treasure Island, Kidnapped, Strange Case of Dr Jekyll and Mr Hyde, and A Child's Garden of Verses. Born and educated in Edinburgh, Stevenson suffered from serious bronchial trouble for much of his life, but continued to write prolifically and travel widely, in defiance of his poor health. As a young man, he mixed in London literary circles, receiving encouragement from Andrew Lang, Edmund Gosse, Leslie Stephen and W. E. Henley, the last of whom may have provided the model for Long John Silver in Treasure Island. His travels took him to France, America and Australia, before he finally settled in Samoa, where he died. A celebrity in his lifetime, Stevenson attracted a more negative critical response for much of the 20th century, though his reputation has been largely restored. He is currently ranked as the 26th most translated author in the world.(Source: Wikipedia)

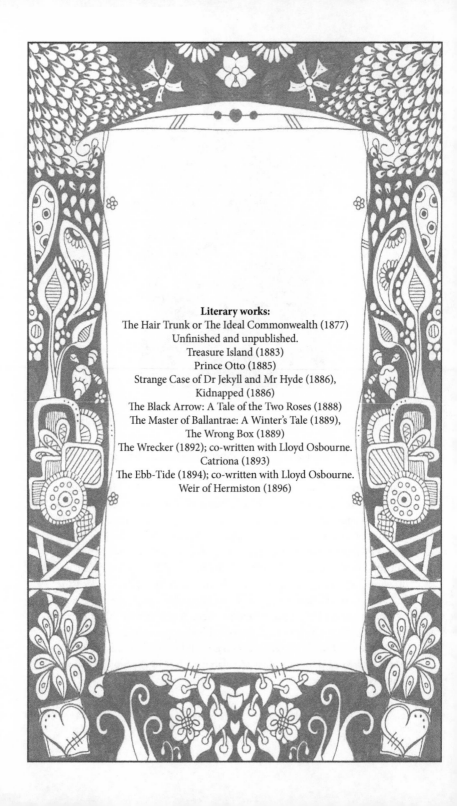

Literary works:
The Hair Trunk or The Ideal Commonwealth (1877)
Unfinished and unpublished.
Treasure Island (1883)
Prince Otto (1885)
Strange Case of Dr Jekyll and Mr Hyde (1886),
Kidnapped (1886)
The Black Arrow: A Tale of the Two Roses (1888)
The Master of Ballantrae: A Winter's Tale (1889),
The Wrong Box (1889)
The Wrecker (1892); co-written with Lloyd Osbourne.
Catriona (1893)
The Ebb-Tide (1894); co-written with Lloyd Osbourne.
Weir of Hermiston (1896)

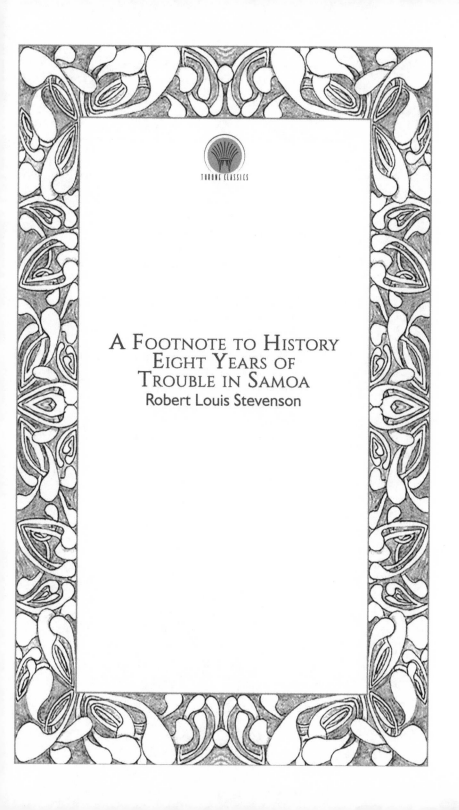

THRONG CLASSICS

A Footnote to History Eight Years of Trouble in Samoa
Robert Louis Stevenson

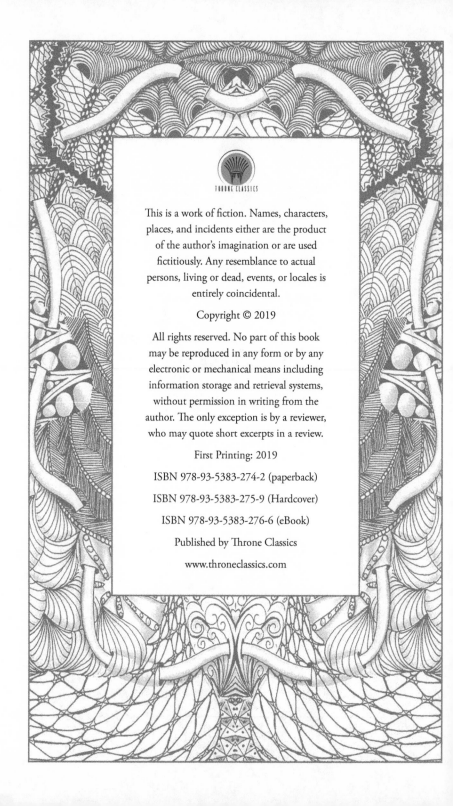

Copyright © 2019

First Printing: 2019

ISBN 978-93-5383-274-2 (paperback)

ISBN 978-93-5383-275-9 (Hardcover)

ISBN 978-93-5383-276-6 (eBook)

Published by Throne Classics

www.throneclassics.com

Contents

A Footnote to History
Eight Years of
Trouble in Samoa

PREFACE

An affair which might be deemed worthy of a note of a few lines in any general history has been here expanded to the size of a volume or large pamphlet. The smallness of the scale, and the singularity of the manners and events and many of the characters, considered, it is hoped that, in spite of its outlandish subject, the sketch may find readers. It has been a task of difficulty. Speed was essential, or it might come too late to be of any service to a distracted country. Truth, in the midst of conflicting rumours and in the dearth of printed material, was often hard to ascertain, and since most of those engaged were of my personal acquaintance, it was often more than delicate to express. I must certainly have erred often and much; it is not for want of trouble taken nor of an impartial temper. And if my plain speaking shall cost me any of the friends that I still count, I shall be sorry, but I need not be ashamed.

In one particular the spelling of Samoan words has been altered; and the characteristic nasal n of the language written throughout ng instead of g. Thus I put Pango-Pango, instead of Pago-Pago; the sound being that of soft ng in English, as in singer, not as in finger.

R. L. S.

VAILIMA,

UPOLU,

SAMOA.

CHAPTER I—THE ELEMENTS OF DISCORD: NATIVE

The story I have to tell is still going on as I write; the characters are alive and active; it is a piece of contemporary history in the most exact sense. And yet, for all its actuality and the part played in it by mails and telegraphs and iron war-ships, the ideas and the manners of the native actors date back before the Roman Empire. They are Christians, church-goers, singers of hymns at family worship, hardy cricketers; their books are printed in London by Spottiswoode, Trübner, or the Tract Society; but in most other points they are the contemporaries of our tattooed ancestors who drove their chariots on the wrong side of the Roman wall. We have passed the feudal system; they are not yet clear of the patriarchal. We are in the thick of the age of finance; they are in a period of communism. And this makes them hard to understand.

To us, with our feudal ideas, Samoa has the first appearance of a land of despotism. An elaborate courtliness marks the race alone among Polynesians; terms of ceremony fly thick as oaths on board a ship; commoners my-lord each other when they meet—and urchins as they play marbles. And for the real noble a whole private dialect is set apart. The common names for an axe, for blood, for bamboo, a bamboo knife, a pig, food, entrails, and an oven are taboo in his presence, as the common names for a bug and for many offices and members of the body are taboo in the drawing-rooms of English ladies. Special words are set apart for his leg, his face, his hair, his belly, his eyelids, his son, his daughter, his wife, his wife's pregnancy, his wife's adultery, adultery with his wife, his dwelling, his spear, his comb, his sleep, his dreams, his anger, the mutual anger of several chiefs, his food, his pleasure in eating, the food and eating of his pigeons, his ulcers, his cough, his sickness, his recovery, his death, his being carried on a bier, the exhumation of his bones, and his skull after death. To address these demigods is quite a branch of knowledge, and he who goes to visit a high chief does well to make sure of the competence of his interpreter. To complete the picture, the same word signifies the watching of a virgin and the warding of a chief; and the same word means to cherish a chief and to fondle a favourite child.

Men like us, full of memories of feudalism, hear of a man so addressed, so flattered, and we leap at once to the conclusion that he is hereditary and absolute. Hereditary he is; born of a great family, he must always be a man of mark; but yet his office is elective and (in a weak sense) is held on good behaviour. Compare the case of a Highland chief: born one of the great ones of his clan, he was sometimes appointed its chief officer and conventional father; was loved, and respected, and served, and fed, and died for implicitly, if he gave loyalty a chance; and yet if he sufficiently outraged clan sentiment, was liable to deposition. As to authority, the parallel is not so close. Doubtless the Samoan chief, if he be popular, wields a great influence; but it is limited. Important matters are debated in a fono, or native parliament, with its feasting and parade, its endless speeches and polite genealogical allusions. Debated, I say—not decided; for even a small minority will often strike a clan or a province impotent. In the midst of these ineffective councils the chief sits usually silent: a kind of a gagged audience for village orators. And the deliverance of the fono seems (for the moment) to be final. The absolute chiefs of Tahiti and Hawaii were addressed as plain John and Thomas; the chiefs of Samoa are surfeited with lip-honour, but the seat and extent of their actual authority is hard to find.

It is so in the members of the state, and worse in the belly. The idea of a sovereign pervades the air; the name we have; the thing we are not so sure of. And the process of election to the chief power is a mystery. Certain provinces have in their gift certain high titles, or names, as they are called. These can only be attributed to the descendants of particular lines. Once granted, each name conveys at once the principality (whatever that be worth) of the province which bestows it, and counts as one suffrage towards the general sovereignty of Samoa. To be indubitable king, they say, or some of them say,—I find few in perfect harmony,—a man should resume five of these names in his own person. But the case is purely hypothetical; local jealousy forbids its occurrence. There are rival provinces, far more concerned in the prosecution of their rivalry than in the choice of a right man for king. If one of these shall have bestowed its name on competitor A, it will be the signal and the sufficient reason for the other to bestow its name on competitor B or C. The majority of Savaii and that of Aana are thus in perennial opposition.

12

Nor is this all. In 1881, Laupepa, the present king, held the three names of Malietoa, Natoaitele, and Tamasoalii; Tamasese held that of Tuiaana; and Mataafa that of Tuiatua. Laupepa had thus a majority of suffrages; he held perhaps as high a proportion as can be hoped in these distracted islands; and he counted among the number the preponderant name of Malietoa. Here, if ever, was an election. Here, if a king were at all possible, was the king. And yet the natives were not satisfied. Laupepa was crowned, March 19th; and next month, the provinces of Aana and Atua met in joint parliament, and elected their own two princes, Tamasese and Mataafa, to an alternate monarchy, Tamasese taking the first trick of two years. War was imminent, when the consuls interfered, and any war were preferable to the terms of the peace which they procured. By the Lackawanna treaty, Laupepa was confirmed king, and Tamasese set by his side in the nondescript office of vice-king. The compromise was not, I am told, without precedent; but it lacked all appearance of success. To the constitution of Samoa, which was already all wheels and no horses, the consuls had added a fifth wheel. In addition to the old conundrum, "Who is the king?" they had supplied a new one, "What is the vice-king?"

Two royal lines; some cloudy idea of alternation between the two; an electorate in which the vote of each province is immediately effectual, as regards itself, so that every candidate who attains one name becomes a perpetual and dangerous competitor for the other four: such are a few of the more trenchant absurdities. Many argue that the whole idea of sovereignty is modern and imported; but it seems impossible that anything so foolish should have been suddenly devised, and the constitution bears on its front the marks of dotage.

But the king, once elected and nominated, what does he become? It may be said he remains precisely as he was. Election to one of the five names is significant; it brings not only dignity but power, and the holder is secure, from that moment, of a certain following in war. But I cannot find that the further step of election to the kingship implies anything worth mention. The successful candidate is now the Tupu o Samoa—much good may it do him! He can so sign himself on proclamations, which it does not follow that any one will heed. He can summon parliaments; it does not follow they will assemble. If he be too flagrantly disobeyed, he can go to war. But so he could before, when he was only the chief of certain provinces. His own provinces will support him, the provinces of his rivals will take the field upon the other part; just as before. In so far as he is the holder of any of the five names, in short, he is a man to be reckoned with; in so far as he is king of Samoa, I cannot find but what the president of a college debating society is a far more formidable officer. And unfortunately, although the credit side of the account proves thus imaginary, the debit side is actual and heavy. For he is now set up to be the mark of consuls; he will be badgered to raise taxes, to make roads, to punish crime, to quell rebellion: and how he is to do it is not asked.

If I am in the least right in my presentation of this obscure matter, no one need be surprised to hear that the land is full of war and rumours of war. Scarce a year goes by but what some province is in arms, or sits sulky and menacing, holding parliaments, disregarding the king's proclamations and planting food in the bush, the first step of military preparation. The religious sentiment of the people is indeed for peace at any price; no pastor can bear arms; and even the layman who does so is denied the sacraments. In the last war the college of Mālua, where the picked youth are prepared for the ministry, lost but a single student; the rest, in the bosom of a bleeding country, and deaf to the voices of vanity and honour, peacefully pursued their studies. But if the church looks askance on war, the warrior in no extremity of need or passion forgets his consideration for the church. The houses and gardens of her ministers stand safe in the midst of armies; a way is reserved for themselves along the beach, where they may be seen in their white kilts and jackets openly passing the lines, while not a hundred yards behind the skirmishers will be exchanging the useless volleys of barbaric warfare. Women are also respected; they are not fired upon; and they are suffered to pass between the hostile camps, exchanging gossip, spreading rumour, and divulging to either army the secret councils of the other. This is plainly no savage war; it has all the punctilio of the barbarian, and all his parade; feasts precede battles, fine dresses and songs decorate and enliven the field; and the young soldier comes to camp burning (on the one hand) to distinguish himself by acts of valour, and (on the other) to display his acquaintance with field etiquette. Thus after Mataafa became involved in hostilities against the Germans, and had another code to observe beside his own, he was always asking his white advisers if "things were done correctly." Let us try to be as wise as Mataafa, and to conceive that etiquette and morals differ in one country and another. We shall be the less surprised to find Samoan war defaced with some unpalatable customs. The childish destruction of fruit-trees in an enemy's country cripples the resources of Samoa; and the habit of head-hunting not only revolts foreigners, but has begun to exercise the minds of the natives themselves. Soon after the German heads were taken, Mr. Carne, Wesleyan missionary, had occasion to visit Mataafa's camp, and spoke of the practice with abhorrence. "Misi Kāne," said one chief, "we have just been puzzling ourselves to guess where that custom came from. But, Misi, is it not so that when David killed Goliath, he cut off his head and carried it before the king?"

With the civil life of the inhabitants we have far less to do; and yet even here a word of preparation is inevitable. They are easy, merry, and pleasure-loving; the gayest, though by far from either the most capable or the most beautiful of Polynesians. Fine dress is a passion, and makes a Samoan festival a thing of beauty. Song is almost ceaseless. The boatman sings at the oar, the family at evening worship, the girls at night in the guest-house, sometimes the workman at his toil. No occasion is too small for the poets and musicians; a death, a visit, the day's news, the day's pleasantry, will be set to rhyme and harmony. Even half-grown girls, the occasion arising, fashion words and train choruses of children for its celebration. Song, as with all Pacific islanders, goes hand in hand with the dance, and both shade into the drama. Some of the performances are indecent and ugly, some only dull; others are pretty, funny, and attractive. Games are popular. Cricket-matches, where a hundred played upon a side, endured at times for weeks, and ate up the country like the presence of an army. Fishing, the daily bath, flirtation; courtship, which is gone upon by proxy; conversation, which is largely political; and the delights of public oratory, fill in the long hours.

But the special delight of the Samoan is the malanga. When people form a party and go from village to village, junketing and gossiping, they are said to go on a malanga. Their songs have announced their approach ere they arrive; the guest-house is prepared for their reception; the virgins of the village attend to prepare the kava bowl and entertain them with the dance; time flies in the enjoyment of every pleasure which an islander conceives; and when the malanga sets forth, the same welcome and the same joys expect them beyond the next cape, where the nearest village nestles in its grove of palms. To the visitors it is all golden; for the hosts, it has another side. In one or two words of the language the fact peeps slyly out. The same word (afemoeina) expresses "a long call" and "to come as a calamity"; the same word (lesolosolou) signifies "to have no intermission of pain" and "to have no cessation, as in the arrival of visitors"; and soua, used of epidemics, bears the sense of being overcome as with "fire, flood, or visitors." But the gem of the dictionary is the verb alovao, which illustrates its pages like a humorous woodcut. It is used in the sense of "to avoid visitors," but it means literally "hide in the wood." So, by the sure hand of popular speech, we have the picture of the house deserted, the malanga disappointed, and the host that should have been quaking in the bush.

We are thus brought to the beginning of a series of traits of manners, highly curious in themselves, and essential to an understanding of the war. In Samoa authority sits on the one hand entranced; on the other, property stands bound in the midst of chartered marauders. What property exists is vested in the family, not in the individual; and of the loose communism in which a family dwells, the dictionary may yet again help us to some idea. I find a string of verbs with the following senses: to deal leniently with, as in helping oneself from a family plantation; to give away without consulting other members of the family; to go to strangers for help instead of to relatives; to take from relatives without permission; to steal from relatives; to have plantations robbed by relatives. The ideal of conduct in the family, and some of its depravations, appear here very plainly. The man who (in a native word of praise) is mata-ainga, a race-regarder, has his hand always open to his kindred; the man who is not (in a native term of contempt) noa, knows always where to turn in any pinch of want or extremity of laziness. Beggary within the family—and by the less self-respecting, without it—has thus grown into a custom and a scourge, and the dictionary teems with evidence of its abuse. Special words signify the begging of food, of uncooked food, of fish, of pigs, of pigs for travellers, of pigs for stock, of taro, of taro-tops, of taro-tops for planting, of tools, of flyhooks, of implements for netting pigeons, and of mats. It is true the beggar was supposed in time to make a return, somewhat as by the Roman contract of mutuum. But the obligation was only moral; it could not be, or was not, enforced; as a matter of fact, it was disregarded. The language had recently to borrow from the Tahitians a word for debt; while by a significant excidence, it possessed a native expression for the failure to pay—"to omit to make a return for property begged." Conceive now the position of the householder besieged by harpies, and all defence denied him by the laws of honour. The sacramental gesture of refusal, his last and single resource, was supposed to signify "my house is destitute." Until that point was reached, in other words, the conduct prescribed for a Samoan was to give and to continue giving. But it does not appear he was at all expected to give with a good grace. The dictionary is well stocked with expressions standing ready, like missiles, to be discharged upon the locusts—"troop of shamefaced ones," "you draw in your head like a tern," "you make your voice small like a whistle-pipe," "you beg like one delirious"; and the verb pongitai, "to look cross," is equipped with the pregnant rider, "as at the sight of beggars."

This insolence of beggars and the weakness of proprietors can only be illustrated by examples. We have a girl in our service to whom we had given some finery, that she might wait at table, and (at her own request) some warm clothing against the cold mornings of the bush. She went on a visit to her family, and returned in an old tablecloth, her whole wardrobe having been divided out among relatives in the course of twenty-four hours. A pastor in the province of Atua, being a handy, busy man, bought a boat for a hundred dollars, fifty of which he paid down. Presently after, relatives came to him upon a visit and took a fancy to his new possession. "We have long been wanting a boat," said they. "Give us this one." So, when the visit was done, they departed in the boat. The pastor, meanwhile, travelled into Savaii the best way he could, sold a parcel of land, and begged mats among his other relatives, to pay the remainder of the price of the boat which was no longer his. You might think this was enough; but some months later, the harpies, having broken a thwart, brought back the boat to be repaired and repainted by the original owner.

Such customs, it might be argued, being double-edged, will ultimately right themselves. But it is otherwise in practice. Such folk as the pastor's harpy relatives will generally have a boat, and will never have paid for it; such men as the pastor may have sometimes paid for a boat, but they will never have one. It is there as it is with us at home: the measure of the abuse of either system is the blackness of the individual heart. The same man, who would drive his poor relatives from his own door in England, would besiege in Samoa the doors of the rich; and the essence of the dishonesty in either case is to pursue one's own advantage and to be indifferent to the losses of one's neighbour. But the particular drawback of the Polynesian system is to depress and stagger industry. To work more is there only to be more pillaged; to save is impossible. The family has then made a good day of it when all are filled and nothing remains over for the crew of free-booters; and the injustice of the system begins to be recognised even in Samoa. One native is said to have amassed a certain fortune; two clever lads have individually expressed to us their discontent with a system which taxes industry to pamper idleness; and I hear that in one village of Savaii a law has been passed forbidding gifts under the penalty of a sharp fine.

Under this economic regimen, the unpopularity of taxes, which strike all at the same time, which expose the industrious to a perfect siege of mendicancy, and the lazy to be actually condemned to a day's labour, may be imagined without words. It is more important to note the concurrent relaxation of all sense of property. From applying for help to kinsmen who are scarce permitted to refuse, it is but a step to taking from them (in the dictionary phrase) "without permission"; from that to theft at large is but a hair's-breadth.

CHAPTER II—THE ELEMENTS OF DISCORD: FOREIGN

The huge majority of Samoans, like other God-fearing folk in other countries, are perfectly content with their own manners. And upon one condition, it is plain they might enjoy themselves far beyond the average of man. Seated in islands very rich in food, the idleness of the many idle would scarce matter; and the provinces might continue to bestow their names among rival pretenders, and fall into war and enjoy that a while, and drop into peace and enjoy that, in a manner highly to be envied. But the condition—that they should be let alone—is now no longer possible. More than a hundred years ago, and following closely on the heels of Cook, an irregular invasion of adventurers began to swarm about the isles of the Pacific. The seven sleepers of Polynesia stand, still but half aroused, in the midst of the century of competition. And the island races, comparable to a shopful of crockery launched upon the stream of time, now fall to make their desperate voyage among pots of brass and adamant.

Apia, the port and mart, is the seat of the political sickness of Samoa. At the foot of a peaked, woody mountain, the coast makes a deep indent, roughly semicircular. In front the barrier reef is broken by the fresh water of the streams; if the swell be from the north, it enters almost without diminution; and the war-ships roll dizzily at their moorings, and along the fringing coral which follows the configuration of the beach, the surf breaks with a continuous uproar. In wild weather, as the world knows, the roads are untenable. Along the whole shore, which is everywhere green and level and overlooked by inland mountain-tops, the town lies drawn out in strings and clusters. The western horn is Mulinuu, the eastern, Matautu; and from one to the other of these extremes, I ask the reader to walk. He will find more of the history of Samoa spread before his eyes in that excursion, than has yet been collected in the blue-books or the white-books of the world. Mulinuu (where the walk is to begin) is a flat, wind-swept promontory, planted with palms, backed against a swamp of mangroves, and occupied by a rather miserable village. The reader is informed that this is the proper residence of the Samoan kings; he will be the more surprised to observe a board set up, and to read that this historic village is the property of the German firm. But these boards, which are among the commonest features of the landscape, may be rather taken to imply that the claim has been disputed. A little farther east he skirts the stores, offices, and barracks of the firm itself. Thence he will pass through Matafele, the one really town-like portion of this long string of villages, by German bars and stores and the German consulate; and reach the Catholic mission and cathedral standing by the mouth of a small river. The bridge which crosses here (bridge of Mulivai) is a frontier; behind is Matafele; beyond, Apia proper; behind, Germans are supreme; beyond, with but few exceptions, all is Anglo-Saxon. Here the reader will go forward past the stores of Mr. Moors (American) and Messrs. MacArthur (English); past the English mission, the office of the English newspaper, the English church, and the old American consulate, till he reaches the mouth of a larger river, the Vaisingano. Beyond, in Matautu, his way takes him in the shade of many trees and by scattered dwellings, and presently brings him beside a great range of offices, the place and the monument of a German who fought the German firm during his life. His house (now he is dead) remains pointed like a discharged cannon at the citadel of his old enemies. Fitly enough, it is at present leased and occupied by Englishmen. A little farther, and the reader gains the eastern flanking angle of the bay, where stands the pilot-house and signal-post, and whence he can see, on the line of the main coast of the island, the British and the new American consulates.

The course of his walk will have been enlivened by a considerable to and fro of pleasure and business. He will have encountered many varieties of whites,—sailors, merchants, clerks, priests, Protestant missionaries in their pith helmets, and the nondescript hangers-on of any island beach. And the sailors are sometimes in considerable force; but not the residents. He will think at times there are more signboards than men to own them. It may chance it is a full day in the harbour; he will then have seen all manner of ships, from men-of-war and deep-sea packets to the labour vessels of the German firm and the cockboat island schooner; and if he be of an arithmetical turn, he may calculate that there are more whites afloat in Apia bay than whites ashore in the whole Archipelago. On the other hand, he will have encountered all ranks of natives, chiefs and pastors in their scrupulous white clothes; perhaps the king himself, attended by guards in uniform; smiling policemen with their pewter stars; girls, women, crowds of cheerful children. And he will have asked himself with some surprise where these reside. Here and there, in the back yards of European establishments, he may have had a glimpse of a native house elbowed in a corner; but since he left Mulinuu, none on the beach where islanders prefer to live, scarce one on the line of street. The handful of whites have everything; the natives walk in a foreign town. A year ago, on a knoll behind a bar-room, he might have observed a native house guarded by sentries and flown over by the standard of Samoa. He would then have been told it was the seat of government, driven (as I have to relate) over the Mulivai and from beyond the German town into the Anglo-Saxon. To-day, he will learn it has been carted back again to its old quarters. And he will think it significant that the king of the islands should be thus shuttled to and fro in his chief city at the nod of aliens. And then he will observe a feature more significant still: a house with some concourse of affairs, policemen and idlers hanging by, a man at a bank-counter overhauling manifests, perhaps a trial proceeding in the front verandah, or perhaps the council breaking up in knots after a stormy sitting. And he will remember that he is in the Eleele Sa, the "Forbidden Soil," or Neutral Territory of the treaties; that the magistrate whom he has just seen trying native criminals is no officer of the native king's; and that this, the only port and place of business in the kingdom, collects and administers its own revenue for its own behoof by the hands of white councillors and under the supervision of white consuls. Let him go further afield. He will find the roads almost everywhere to cease or to be made impassable by native pig-fences, bridges to be quite unknown, and houses of the whites to become at once a rare exception. Set aside the German plantations, and the frontier is sharp. At the boundary of the Eleele Sa, Europe ends, Samoa begins. Here, then, is a singular state of affairs: all the money, luxury, and business of the kingdom centred in one place; that place excepted from the native government and administered by whites for whites; and the whites themselves holding it not in common but in hostile camps, so that it lies between them like a bone between two dogs, each growling, each clutching his own end.

Should Apia ever choose a coat of arms, I have a motto ready: "Enter Rumour painted full of tongues." The majority of the natives do extremely little; the majority of the whites are merchants with some four mails in the month, shopkeepers with some ten or twenty customers a day, and gossip is the common resource of all. The town hums to the day's news, and the bars are crowded with amateur politicians. Some are office-seekers, and earwig king and consul, and compass the fall of officials, with an eye to salary. Some are humorists, delighted with the pleasure of faction for itself. "I never saw so good a place as this Apia," said one of these; "you can be in a new conspiracy every day!" Many, on the other hand, are sincerely concerned for the future of the country. The quarters are so close and the scale is so small, that perhaps not any one can be trusted always to preserve his temper. Every one tells everything he knows; that is our country sickness. Nearly every one has been betrayed at times, and told a trifle more; the way our sickness takes the predisposed. And the news flies, and the tongues wag, and fists are shaken. Pot boil and caldron bubble!

Within the memory of man, the white people of Apia lay in the worst squalor of degradation. They are now unspeakably improved, both men and women. To-day they must be called a more than fairly respectable population, and a much more than fairly intelligent. The whole would probably not fill the ranks of even an English half-battalion, yet there are a surprising number above the average in sense, knowledge, and manners. The trouble (for Samoa) is that they are all here after a livelihood. Some are sharp practitioners, some are famous (justly or not) for foul play in business. Tales fly. One merchant warns you against his neighbour; the neighbour on the first occasion is found to return the compliment: each with a good circumstantial story to the proof. There is so much copra in the islands, and no more; a man's share of it is his share of bread; and commerce, like politics, is here narrowed to a focus, shows its ugly side, and becomes as personal as fisticuffs. Close at their elbows, in all this contention, stands the native looking on. Like a child, his true analogue, he observes, apprehends, misapprehends, and is usually silent. As in a child, a considerable intemperance of speech is accompanied by some power of secrecy. News he publishes; his thoughts have often to be dug for. He looks on at the rude career of the dollar-hunt, and wonders. He sees these men rolling in a luxury beyond the ambition of native kings; he hears them accused by each other of the meanest trickery; he knows some of them to be guilty; and what is he to think? He is strongly conscious of his own position as the common milk-cow; and what is he to do? "Surely these white men on the beach are not great chiefs?" is a common question, perhaps asked with some design of flattering the person questioned. And one, stung by the last incident into an unusual flow of English, remarked to me: "I begin to be weary of white men on the beach."

But the true centre of trouble, the head of the boil of which Samoa languishes, is the German firm. From the conditions of business, a great island house must ever be an inheritance of care; and it chances that the greatest still afoot has its chief seat in Apia bay, and has sunk the main part of its capital in the island of Upolu. When its founder, John Cæsar Godeffroy, went bankrupt over Russian paper and Westphalian iron, his most considerable asset was found to be the South Sea business. This passed (I understand) through the hands of Baring Brothers in London, and is now run by a company rejoicing in the Gargantuan name of the Deutsche Handels und Plantagen Gesellschaft für Süd-See Inseln zu Hamburg. This piece of literature is (in practice) shortened to the D. H. and P. G., the Old Firm, the German Firm, the Firm, and (among humorists) the Long Handle Firm. Even from the deck of an approaching ship, the island is seen to bear its signature—zones of cultivation showing in a more vivid tint of green on the dark vest of forest. The total area in use is near ten thousand acres. Hedges of fragrant lime enclose, broad avenues intersect them. You shall walk for hours in parks of palm-tree alleys, regular, like soldiers on parade; in the recesses of the hills you may stumble on a mill-house, toiling and trembling there, fathoms deep in superincumbent forest. On the carpet of clean sward, troops of horses and herds of handsome cattle may be seen to browse; and to one accustomed to the rough luxuriance of the tropics, the appearance is of fairyland. The managers, many of them German sea-captains, are enthusiastic in their new employment. Experiment is continually afoot: coffee and cacao, both of excellent quality, are among the more recent outputs; and from one plantation quantities of pineapples are sent at a particular season to the Sydney markets. A hundred and fifty thousand pounds of English money, perhaps two hundred thousand, lie sunk in these magnificent estates. In estimating the expense of maintenance quite a fleet of ships must be remembered, and a strong staff of captains, supercargoes, overseers, and clerks. These last mess together at a liberal board; the wages are high, and the staff is inspired with a strong and pleasing sentiment of loyalty to their employers.

Seven or eight hundred imported men and women toil for the company on contracts of three or of five years, and at a hypothetical wage of a few dollars in the month. I am now on a burning question: the labour traffic; and I shall ask permission in this place only to touch it with the tongs. Suffice it to say that in Queensland, Fiji, New Caledonia, and Hawaii it has been either suppressed or placed under close public supervision. In Samoa, where it still flourishes, there is no regulation of which the public receives any evidence; and the dirty linen of the firm, if there be any dirty, and if it be ever washed at all, is washed in private. This is unfortunate, if Germans would believe it. But they have no idea of publicity, keep their business to themselves, rather affect to "move in a mysterious way," and are naturally incensed by criticisms, which they consider hypocritical, from men who would import "labour" for themselves, if they could afford it, and would probably maltreat them if they dared. It is said the whip is very busy on some of the plantations; it is said that punitive extra-labour, by which the thrall's term of service is extended, has grown to be an abuse; and it is complained that, even where that term is out, much irregularity occurs in the repatriation of the discharged. To all this I can say nothing, good or bad. A certain number of the thralls, many of them wild negritos from the west, have taken to the bush, harbour there in a state partly bestial, or creep into the back quarters of the town to do a day's stealthy labour under the nose of their proprietors. Twelve were arrested one morning in my own boys' kitchen. Farther in the bush, huts, small patches of cultivation, and smoking ovens, have been found by hunters. There are still three runaways in the woods of Tutuila, whither they escaped upon a raft. And the Samoans regard these dark-skinned rangers with extreme alarm; the fourth refugee in Tutuila was shot down (as I was told in that island) while carrying off the virgin of a village; and tales of cannibalism run round the country, and the natives shudder about the evening fire. For the Samoans are not cannibals, do not seem to remember when they were, and regard the practice with a disfavour equal to our own.

The firm is Gulliver among the Lilliputs; and it must not be forgotten, that while the small, independent traders are fighting for their own hand, and inflamed with the usual jealousy against corporations, the Germans are inspired with a sense of the greatness of their affairs and interests. The thought of the money sunk, the sight of these costly and beautiful plantations, menaced yearly by the returning forest, and the responsibility of administering with one hand so many conjunct fortunes, might well nerve the manager of such a company for desperate and questionable deeds. Upon this scale, commercial sharpness has an air of patriotism; and I can imagine the man, so far from haggling over the scourge for a few Solomon islanders, prepared to oppress rival firms, overthrow inconvenient monarchs, and let loose the dogs of war. Whatever he may decide, he will not want for backing. Every clerk will be eager to be up and strike a blow; and most Germans in the group, whatever they may babble of the firm over the walnuts and the wine, will rally round the national concern at the approach of difficulty. They are so few—I am ashamed to give their number, it were to challenge contradiction— they are so few, and the amount of national capital buried at their feet is so vast, that we must not wonder if they seem oppressed with greatness and the sense of empire. Other whites take part in our brabbles, while temper holds out, with a certain schoolboy entertainment. In the Germans alone, no trace of humour is to be observed, and their solemnity is accompanied by a touchiness often beyond belief. Patriotism flies in arms about a hen; and if you comment upon the colour of a Dutch umbrella, you have cast a stone against the German Emperor. I give one instance, typical although extreme. One who had returned from Tutuila on the mail cutter complained of the vermin with which she is infested. He was suddenly and sharply brought to a stand. The ship of which he spoke, he was reminded, was a German ship.

John Cæsar Godeffroy himself had never visited the islands; his sons and nephews came, indeed, but scarcely to reap laurels; and the mainspring and headpiece of this great concern, until death took him, was a certain remarkable man of the name of Theodor Weber. He was of an artful and commanding character; in the smallest thing or the greatest, without fear or scruple; equally able to affect, equally ready to adopt, the most engaging politeness or the most imperious airs of domination. It was he who did most damage to rival traders; it was he who most harried the Samoans; and yet I never met any one, white or native, who did not respect his memory. All felt it was a gallant battle, and the man a great fighter; and now when he is dead, and the war seems to have gone against him, many can scarce remember, without a kind of regret, how much devotion and audacity have been spent in vain. His name still lives in the songs of Samoa. One, that I have heard, tells of Misi Ueba and a biscuit-box—the suggesting incident being long since forgotten. Another sings plaintively how all things, land and food and property, pass progressively, as by a law of nature, into the hands of Misi Ueba, and soon nothing will be left for Samoans. This is an epitaph the man would have enjoyed.

At one period of his career, Weber combined the offices of director of the firm and consul for the City of Hamburg. No question but he then drove very hard. Germans admit that the combination was unfortunate; and it was a German who procured its overthrow. Captain Zembsch superseded him with an imperial appointment, one still remembered in Samoa as "the gentleman who acted justly." There was no house to be found, and the new consul must take up his quarters at first under the same roof with Weber. On several questions, in which the firm was vitally interested, Zembsch embraced the contrary opinion. Riding one day with an Englishman in Vailele plantation, he was startled by a burst of screaming, leaped from the saddle, ran round a house, and found an overseer beating one of the thralls. He punished the overseer, and, being a kindly and perhaps not a very diplomatic man, talked high of what he felt and what he might consider it his duty to forbid or to enforce. The firm began to look askance at such a consul; and worse was behind. A number of deeds being brought to the consulate for registration, Zembsch detected certain transfers of land in which the date, the boundaries, the measure, and the consideration were all blank. He refused them with an indignation which he does not seem to have been able to keep to himself; and, whether or not by his fault, some of these unfortunate documents became public. It was plain that the relations between the two flanks of the German invasion, the diplomatic and the commercial, were strained to bursting. But

Weber was a man ill to conquer. Zembsch was recalled; and from that time forth, whether through influence at home, or by the solicitations of Weber on the spot, the German consulate has shown itself very apt to play the game of the German firm. That game, we may say, was twofold,—the first part even praiseworthy, the second at least natural. On the one part, they desired an efficient native administration, to open up the country and punish crime; they wished, on the other, to extend their own provinces and to curtail the dealings of their rivals. In the first, they had the jealous and diffident sympathy of all whites; in the second, they had all whites banded together against them for their lives and livelihoods. It was thus a game of Beggar my Neighbour between a large merchant and some small ones. Had it so remained, it would still have been a cut-throat quarrel. But when the consulate appeared to be concerned, when the war-ships of the German Empire were thought to fetch and carry for the firm, the rage of the independent traders broke beyond restraint. And, largely from the national touchiness and the intemperate speech of German clerks, this scramble among dollar-hunters assumed the appearance of an inter-racial war.

The firm, with the indomitable Weber at its head and the consulate at its back—there has been the chief enemy at Samoa. No English reader can fail to be reminded of John Company; and if the Germans appear to have been not so successful, we can only wonder that our own blunders and brutalities were less severely punished. Even on the field of Samoa, though German faults and aggressors make up the burthen of my story, they have been nowise alone. Three nations were engaged in this infinitesimal affray, and not one appears with credit. They figure but as the three ruffians of the elder play-wrights. The United States have the cleanest hands, and even theirs are not immaculate. It was an ambiguous business when a private American adventurer was landed with his pieces of artillery from an American war-ship, and became prime minister to the king. It is true (even if he were ever really supported) that he was soon dropped and had soon sold himself for money to the German firm. I will leave it to the reader whether this trait dignifies or not the wretched story. And the end of it spattered the credit alike of England and the States, when this man (the premier of a friendly sovereign) was kidnapped and deported, on the requisition of an American consul, by

27

the captain of an English war-ship. I shall have to tell, as I proceed, of villages shelled on very trifling grounds by Germans; the like has been done of late years, though in a better quarrel, by ourselves of England. I shall have to tell how the Germans landed and shed blood at Fangalii; it was only in 1876 that we British had our own misconceived little massacre at Mulinuu. I shall have to tell how the Germans bludgeoned Malietoa with a sudden call for money; it was something of the suddenest that Sir Arthur Gordon himself, smarting under a sensible public affront, made and enforced a somewhat similar demand.

CHAPTER III—THE SORROWS OF LAUPEPA, 1883 TO 1887

You ride in a German plantation and see no bush, no soul stirring; only acres of empty sward, miles of cocoa-nut alley: a desert of food. In the eyes of the Samoan the place has the attraction of a park for the holiday schoolboy, of a granary for mice. We must add the yet more lively allurement of a haunted house, for over these empty and silent miles there broods the fear of the negrito cannibal. For the Samoan besides, there is something barbaric, unhandsome, and absurd in the idea of thus growing food only to send it from the land and sell it. A man at home who should turn all Yorkshire into one wheatfield, and annually burn his harvest on the altar of Mumbo-Jumbo, might impress ourselves not much otherwise. And the firm which does these things is quite extraneous, a wen that might be excised to-morrow without loss but to itself; few natives drawing from it so much as day's wages; and the rest beholding in it only the occupier of their acres. The nearest villages have suffered most; they see over the hedge the lands of their ancestors waving with useless cocoa-palms; and the sales were often questionable, and must still more often appear so to regretful natives, spinning and improving yarns about the evening lamp. At the worst, then, to help oneself from the plantation will seem to a Samoan very like orchard-breaking to the British schoolboy; at the best, it will be thought a gallant Robin-Hoodish readjustment of a public wrong.

And there is more behind. Not only is theft from the plantations regarded rather as a lark and peccadillo, the idea of theft in itself is not very clearly present to these communists; and as to the punishment of crime in general, a great gulf of opinion divides the natives from ourselves. Indigenous punishments were short and sharp. Death, deportation by the primitive method of setting the criminal to sea in a canoe, fines, and in Samoa itself the penalty of publicly biting a hot, ill-smelling root, comparable to a rough forfeit in a children's game—these are approved. The offender is killed, or punished and forgiven. We, on the other hand, harbour malice for a period of years: continuous shame attaches to the criminal; even when he is doing his best—even when he is submitting to the worst form of torture, regular work—he is to stand aside from life and from his family in dreadful isolation. These ideas most Polynesians have accepted in appearance, as they accept other ideas of the whites; in practice, they reduce it to a farce. I have heard the French resident in the Marquesas in talk with the French gaoler of Tai-o-hae: "Eh bien, où sont vos prisonnières?—Je crois, mon commandant, qu'elles sont allées quelque part faire une visite." And the ladies would be welcome. This is to take the most savage of Polynesians; take some of the most civilised. In Honolulu, convicts labour on the highways in piebald clothing, gruesome and ridiculous; and it is a common sight to see the family of such an one troop out, about the dinner hour, wreathed with flowers and in their holiday best, to picnic with their kinsman on the public wayside. The application of these outlandish penalties, in fact, transfers the sympathy to the offender. Remember, besides, that the clan system, and that imperfect idea of justice which is its worst feature, are still lively in Samoa; that it is held the duty of a judge to favour kinsmen, of a king to protect his vassals; and the difficulty of getting a plantation thief first caught, then convicted, and last of all punished, will appear.

During the early 'eighties, the Germans looked upon this system with growing irritation. They might see their convict thrust in gaol by the front door; they could never tell how soon he was enfranchised by the back; and they need not be the least surprised if they met him, a few days after, enjoying the delights of a malanga. It was a banded conspiracy, from the king and the vice-king downward, to evade the law and deprive the Germans of their profits. In 1883, accordingly, the consul, Dr. Stuebel, extorted a convention on the subject, in terms of which Samoans convicted of offences against German subjects were to be confined in a private gaol belonging to the German firm. To Dr. Stuebel it seemed simple enough: the offenders were to be effectually punished, the sufferers partially indemnified. To the Samoans, the thing appeared no less simple, but quite different: "Malietoa was selling Samoans to Misi Ueba." What else could be expected? Here was a private corporation engaged in making money; to it was delegated, upon a question of profit and loss, one of the functions of the Samoan crown; and those who make anomalies must look for comments. Public feeling ran unanimous and high. Prisoners who escaped from the private gaol were not recaptured or not returned and Malietoa hastened to build a new prison of his own, whither he conveyed, or pretended to convey, the fugitives. In October 1885 a trenchant state paper issued from the German consulate. Twenty prisoners, the consul wrote, had now been at large for eight months from Weber's prison. It was pretended they had since then completed their term of punishment elsewhere. Dr. Stuebel did not seek to conceal his incredulity; but he took ground beyond; he declared the point irrelevant. The law was to be enforced. The men were condemned to a certain period in Weber's prison; they had run away; they must now be brought back and (whatever had become of them in the interval) work out the sentence. Doubtless Dr. Stuebel's demands were substantially just; but doubtless also they bore from the outside a great appearance of harshness; and when the king submitted, the murmurs of the people increased.

But Weber was not yet content. The law had to be enforced; property, or at least the property of the firm, must be respected. And during an absence of the consul's, he seems to have drawn up with his own hand, and certainly first showed to the king, in his own house, a new convention. Weber here and Weber there. As an able man, he was perhaps in the right to prepare and propose conventions. As the head of a trading company, he seems far out of his part to be communicating state papers to a sovereign. The administration of justice was the colour, and I am willing to believe the purpose, of the new paper; but its effect was to depose the existing government. A council of two Germans and two Samoans were to be invested with the right to make laws and impose taxes as might be "desirable for the common interest of the Samoan government and the German residents." The provisions of this council the king and vice-king were to sign blindfold. And by a last hardship, the Germans, who received all the benefit, reserved a right to recede from the agreement on six months' notice; the Samoans, who suffered all the loss, were bound by it in perpetuity. I can never believe that my friend Dr. Stuebel had a hand in drafting these proposals; I am only surprised he should have been a party to enforcing them, perhaps the chief error in these islands of a man who has made few. And they were enforced with a rigour that seems injudicious. The Samoans (according to their own account) were denied a copy of the document; they were certainly rated and threatened; their deliberation was treated as contumacy; two German war-ships lay in port, and it was hinted that these would shortly intervene.

Succeed in frightening a child, and he takes refuge in duplicity. "Malietoa," one of the chiefs had written, "we know well we are in bondage to the great governments." It was now thought one tyrant might be better than three, and any one preferable to Germany. On the 5th November 1885, accordingly, Laupepa, Tamasese, and forty-eight high chiefs met in secret, and the supremacy of Samoa was secretly offered to Great Britain for the second time in history. Laupepa and Tamasese still figured as king and vice-king in the eyes of Dr. Stuebel; in their own, they had secretly abdicated, were become private persons, and might do what they pleased without binding or dishonouring their country. On the morrow, accordingly, they did public humiliation in the dust before the consulate, and five days later signed the convention. The last was done, it is claimed, upon an impulse. The humiliation, which it appeared to the Samoans so great a thing to offer, to the practical mind of Dr. Stuebel seemed a trifle to receive; and the pressure was continued and increased. Laupepa and Tamasese were both heavy, well-meaning, inconclusive men. Laupepa, educated for the ministry, still bears some marks of it in character and appearance; Tamasese was in private of an amorous and sentimental turn, but no one would have guessed it from his solemn and dull countenance. Impossible to conceive two less dashing champions for a threatened race; and there is no doubt they were reduced to the extremity of muddlement and childish fear. It was drawing towards night on the 10th, when this luckless pair and a chief of the name of Tuiatafu, set out for the German consulate, still minded to temporise. As they went, they discussed their case with agitation. They could see the lights of the German war-ships as they walked—an eloquent reminder. And it was then that Tamasese proposed to sign the convention. "It will give us peace for the day," said Laupepa, "and afterwards Great Britain must decide."—"Better fight Germany than that!" cried Tuiatafu, speaking words of wisdom, and departed in anger. But the two others proceeded on their fatal errand; signed the convention, writing themselves king and vice-king, as they now believed themselves to be no longer; and with childish perfidy took part in a scene of "reconciliation" at the German consulate.

Malietoa supposed himself betrayed by Tamasese. Consul Churchward states with precision that the document was sold by a scribe for thirty-six dollars. Twelve days later at least, November 22nd, the text of the address to Great Britain came into the hands of Dr. Stuebel. The Germans may have been wrong before; they were now in the right to be angry. They had been publicly, solemnly, and elaborately fooled; the treaty and the reconciliation were both fraudulent, with the broad, farcical fraudulency of children and barbarians. This history is much from the outside; it is the digested report of eye-witnesses; it can be rarely corrected from state papers; and as to what consuls felt and thought, or what instructions they acted under, I must still be silent or proceed by guess. It is my guess that Stuebel now decided Malietoa Laupepa to be a man impossible to trust and unworthy to be dealt with. And it is certain that the business of his deposition was put in hand at once. The position of Weber, with his knowledge of things native, his prestige, and his enterprising intellect, must have always made him influential with the consul: at this juncture he was indispensable. Here was the deed to be done; here the man of action. "Mr. Weber rested not," says Laupepa. It was "like the old days of his own consulate," writes Churchward. His messengers filled the isle; his house was thronged with chiefs and orators; he sat close over his loom, delightedly weaving the future. There was one thing requisite to the intrigue,—a native pretender; and the very man, you would have said, stood waiting: Mataafa, titular of Atua, descended from both the royal lines, late joint king with Tamasese, fobbed off with nothing in the time of the Lackawanna treaty, probably mortified by the circumstance, a chief with a strong following, and in character and capacity high above the native average. Yet when Weber's spiriting was done, and the curtain rose on the set scene of the coronation, Mataafa was absent, and Tamasese stood in his place. Malietoa was to be deposed for a piece of solemn and offensive trickery, and the man selected to replace him was his sole partner and accomplice in the act. For so strange a choice, good ground must have existed; but it remains conjectural: some supposing Mataafa scratched as too independent; others that Tamasese had indeed betrayed Laupepa, and his new advancement was the price of his treachery.

So these two chiefs began to change places like the scales of a balance, one down, the other up. Tamasese raised his flag (Jan. 28th, 1886) in Leulumoenga, chief place of his own province of Aana, usurped the style of king, and began to collect and arm a force. Weber, by the admission of Stuebel, was in the market supplying him with weapons; so were the Americans; so, but for our salutary British law, would have been the British; for wherever there is a sound of battle, there will the traders be gathered together selling arms. A little longer, and we find Tamasese visited and addressed as king and majesty by a German commodore. Meanwhile, for the unhappy Malietoa, the road led downward. He was refused a bodyguard. He was turned out of Mulinuu, the seat of his royalty, on a land claim of Weber's, fled across the Mulivai, and "had the coolness" (German expression) to hoist his flag in Apia. He was asked "in the most polite manner," says the same account—"in the most delicate manner in the world," a reader of Marryat might be tempted to amend the phrase,—to strike his flag in his own capital; and on his "refusal to accede to this request," Dr. Stuebel appeared himself with ten men and an officer from the cruiser Albatross; a sailor climbed into the tree and brought down the flag of Samoa, which was carefully folded, and sent, "in the most polite manner," to its owner. The consuls of England and the States were there (the excellent gentlemen!) to protest. Last, and yet more explicit, the German commodore who visited the be-titled Tamasese, addressed the king—we may surely say the late king—as "the High Chief Malietoa."

Had he no party, then? At that time, it is probable, he might have called some five-sevenths of Samoa to his standard. And yet he sat there, helpless monarch, like a fowl trussed for roasting. The blame lies with himself, because he was a helpless creature; it lies also with England and the States. Their agents on the spot preached peace (where there was no peace, and no pretence of it) with eloquence and iteration. Secretary Bayard seems to have felt a call to join personally in the solemn farce, and was at the expense of a telegram in which he assured the sinking monarch it was "for the higher interests of Samoa" he should do nothing. There was no man better at doing that; the advice came straight home, and was devoutly followed. And to be just to the great Powers, something was done in Europe; a conference was called, it was agreed to send commissioners to Samoa, and the decks had to be hastily cleared against their visit. Dr. Stuebel had attached the municipality of Apia and hoisted the German war-flag over Mulinuu; the American consul (in a sudden access of good service) had flown the stars and stripes over Samoan colours; on either side these steps were solemnly retracted. The Germans expressly disowned Tamasese; and the islands fell into a period of suspense, of some twelve months' duration, during which the seat of the history was transferred to other countries and escapes my purview. Here on the spot, I select three incidents: the arrival on the scene of a new actor, the visit of the Hawaiian embassy, and the riot on the Emperor's birthday. The rest shall be silence; only it must be borne in view that Tamasese all the while continued to strengthen himself in Leulumoenga, and Laupepa sat inactive listening to the song of consuls.

Captain Brandeis. The new actor was Brandeis, a Bavarian captain of artillery, of a romantic and adventurous character. He had served with credit in war; but soon wearied of garrison life, resigned his battery, came to the States, found employment as a civil engineer, visited Cuba, took a sub-contract on the Panama canal, caught the fever, and came (for the sake of the sea voyage) to Australia. He had that natural love for the tropics which lies so often latent in persons of a northern birth; difficulty and danger attracted him; and when he was picked out for secret duty, to be the hand of Germany in Samoa, there is no doubt but he accepted the post with exhilaration. It is doubtful if a better choice could have been made. He had courage, integrity, ideas of his own, and loved the employment, the people, and the place. Yet there was a fly in the ointment. The double error of unnecessary stealth and of the immixture of a trading company in political affairs, has vitiated, and in the end defeated, much German policy. And Brandeis was introduced to the islands as a clerk, and sent down to Leulumoenga (where he was soon drilling the troops and fortifying the position of the rebel king) as an agent of the German firm. What this mystification cost in the end I shall tell in another place; and even in the beginning, it deceived no one. Brandeis is a man of notable personal appearance; he looks the part allotted him; and the military clerk was soon the centre of observation and rumour. Malietoa wrote and complained of his presence to Becker, who had succeeded Dr. Stuebel in the consulate. Becker replied, "I have nothing to do with the gentleman Brandeis. Be it well known that the gentleman Brandeis has no appointment in a military character, but resides peaceably assisting the government of Leulumoenga in their work, for Brandeis is a quiet, sensible gentleman." And then he promised to send the vice-consul to "get information of the captain's doings": surely supererogation of deceit.

The Hawaiian Embassy. The prime minister of the Hawaiian kingdom was, at this period, an adventurer of the name of Gibson. He claimed, on the strength of a romantic story, to be the heir of a great English house. He had played a part in a revolt in Java, had languished in Dutch fetters, and had risen to be a trusted agent of Brigham Young, the Utah president. It was in this character of a Mormon emissary that he first came to the islands of Hawaii, where he collected a large sum of money for the Church of the Latter Day Saints. At a given moment, he dropped his saintship and appeared as a Christian and the owner of a part of the island of Lanai. The steps of the transformation are obscure; they seem, at least, to have been ill-received at Salt Lake; and there is evidence to the effect that he was followed to the islands by Mormon assassins. His first attempt on politics was made under the auspices of what is called the missionary party, and the canvass conducted largely (it is said with tears) on the platform at prayer-meetings. It resulted in defeat. Without any decency of delay he changed his colours, abjured the errors of reform, and, with the support of the Catholics, rose to the chief power. In a very brief interval he had thus run through the gamut of religions in the South Seas. It does not appear that he was any more particular in politics, but he was careful to consult the character and prejudices of the late king, Kalakaua. That amiable, far from unaccomplished, but too convivial sovereign, had a continued use for money: Gibson was observant to keep him well supplied. Kalakaua (one of the most theoretical of men) was filled with visionary schemes for the protection and development of the Polynesian race: Gibson fell in step with him; it is even thought he may have shared in his illusions. The king and minister at least conceived between them a scheme of island confederation—the most obvious fault of which was that it came too late—and armed and fitted out the cruiser Kaimiloa, nest-egg of the future navy of Hawaii. Samoa, the most important group still independent, and one immediately threatened with aggression, was chosen for the scene of action. The Hon. John E. Bush, a half-caste Hawaiian, sailed (December

1887) for Apia as minister-plenipotentiary, accompanied by a secretary of legation, Henry F. Poor; and as soon as she was ready for sea, the war-ship followed in support. The expedition was futile in its course, almost tragic in result. The Kaimiloa was from the first a scene of disaster and dilapidation: the stores were sold; the crew revolted; for a great part of a night she was in the hands of mutineers, and the secretary lay bound upon the deck. The mission, installing itself at first with extravagance in Matautu, was helped at last out of the island by the advances of a private citizen. And they returned from dreams of Polynesian independence to find their own city in the hands of a clique of white shopkeepers, and the great Gibson once again in gaol. Yet the farce had not been quite without effect. It had encouraged the natives for the moment, and it seems to have ruffled permanently the temper of the Germans. So might a fly irritate Cæsar.

The arrival of a mission from Hawaii would scarce affect the composure of the courts of Europe. But in the eyes of Polynesians the little kingdom occupies a place apart. It is there alone that men of their race enjoy most of the advantages and all the pomp of independence; news of Hawaii and descriptions of Honolulu are grateful topics in all parts of the South Seas; and there is no better introduction than a photograph in which the bearer shall be represented in company with Kalakaua. Laupepa was, besides, sunk to the point at which an unfortunate begins to clutch at straws, and he received the mission with delight. Letters were exchanged between him and Kalakaua; a deed of confederation was signed, 17th February 1887, and the signature celebrated in the new house of the Hawaiian embassy with some original ceremonies. Malietoa Laupepa came, attended by his ministry, several hundred chiefs, two guards, and six policemen. Always decent, he withdrew at an early hour; by those that remained, all decency appears to have been forgotten; high chiefs were seen to dance; and day found the house carpeted with slumbering grandees, who must be roused, doctored with coffee, and sent home. As a first chapter in the history of Polynesian Confederation, it was hardly cheering, and Laupepa remarked to one of the embassy, with equal dignity and sense: "If you have come here to teach my people to drink, I wish you had stayed away."

The Germans looked on from the first with natural irritation that a power of the powerlessness of Hawaii should thus profit by its undeniable footing in the family of nations, and send embassies, and make believe to have a navy, and bark and snap at the heels of the great German Empire. But Becker could not prevent the hunted Laupepa from taking refuge in any hole that offered, and he could afford to smile at the fantastic orgie in the embassy. It was another matter when the Hawaiians approached the intractable Mataafa, sitting still in his Atua government like Achilles in his tent, helping neither side, and (as the Germans suspected) keeping the eggs warm for himself. When the Kaimiloa steamed out of Apia on this visit, the German war-ship Adler followed at her heels; and Mataafa was no sooner set down with the embassy than he was summoned and ordered on board by two German officers. The step is one of those triumphs of temper which can only be admired. Mataafa is entertaining the plenipotentiary of a sovereign power in treaty with his own king, and the captain of a German corvette orders him to quit his guests.

But there was worse to come. I gather that Tamasese was at the time in the sulks. He had doubtless been promised prompt aid and a prompt success; he had seen himself surreptitiously helped, privately ordered about, and publicly disowned; and he was still the king of nothing more than his own province, and already the second in command of Captain Brandeis. With the adhesion of some part of his native cabinet, and behind the back of his white minister, he found means to communicate with the Hawaiians. A passage on the Kaimiloa, a pension, and a home in Honolulu were the bribes proposed; and he seems to have been tempted. A day was set for a secret interview. Poor, the Hawaiian secretary, and J. D. Strong, an American painter attached to the embassy in the surprising quality of "Government Artist," landed with a Samoan boat's-crew in Aana; and while the secretary hid himself, according to agreement, in the outlying home of an English settler, the artist (ostensibly bent on photography) entered the headquarters of the rebel king. It was a great day in Leulumoenga; three hundred recruits had come in, a feast was cooking; and the photographer, in view of the native love of being photographed, was made entirely welcome. But beneath the friendly surface all were on the alert. The secret had leaked out: Weber beheld his plans threatened in the root; Brandeis trembled for the possession of his slave and sovereign; and the German vice-consul, Mr. Sonnenschein, had been sent or summoned to the scene of danger.

It was after dark, prayers had been said and the hymns sung through all the village, and Strong and the German sat together on the mats in the house of Tamasese, when the events began. Strong speaks German freely, a fact which he had not disclosed, and he was scarce more amused than embarrassed to be able to follow all the evening the dissension and the changing counsels of his neighbours. First the king himself was missing, and there was a false alarm that he had escaped and was already closeted with Poor. Next came certain intelligence that some of the ministry had run the blockade, and were on their way to the house of the English settler. Thereupon, in spite of some protests from Tamasese, who tried to defend the independence of his cabinet, Brandeis gathered a posse of warriors, marched out of the village, brought back the fugitives, and clapped them in the corrugated iron shanty which served as gaol. Along with these he seems to have seized Billy Coe, interpreter to the Hawaiians; and Poor, seeing his conspiracy public, burst with his boat's-crew into the town, made his way to the house of the native prime minister, and demanded Coe's release. Brandeis hastened to the spot, with Strong at his heels; and the two principals being both incensed, and Strong seriously alarmed for his friend's safety, there began among them a scene of great intemperance. At one point, when Strong suddenly disclosed his acquaintance with German, it attained a high style of comedy; at another, when a pistol was most foolishly drawn, it bordered on drama; and it may be said to have ended in a mixed genus, when Poor was finally packed into the corrugated iron gaol along with the forfeited ministers. Meanwhile the captain of his boat, Siteoni, of whom I shall have to tell again, had cleverly withdrawn the boat's-crew at an early stage of the quarrel. Among the population beyond Tamasese's marches, he collected a body of armed men, returned before dawn to Leulumoenga, demolished the corrugated iron gaol, and liberated the Hawaiian secretary and the rump of the rebel cabinet. No opposition was shown; and doubtless the rescue was connived at by Brandeis, who had gained his point. Poor had the face to complain the next day to Becker; but to compete with Becker in effrontery was labour lost. "You have been repeatedly warned, Mr. Poor, not to expose yourself among these savages," said he.

Not long after, the presence of the Kaimiloa was made a casus belli by the Germans; and the rough-and-tumble embassy withdrew, on borrowed money, to find their own government in hot water to the neck.

* * * * *

The Emperor's Birthday. It is possible, and it is alleged, that the Germans entered into the conference with hope. But it is certain they were resolved to remain prepared for either fate. And I take the liberty of believing that Laupepa was not forgiven his duplicity; that, during this interval, he stood marked like a tree for felling; and that his conduct was daily scrutinised for further pretexts of offence. On the evening of the Emperor's birthday, March 22nd, 1887, certain Germans were congregated in a public bar. The season and the place considered, it is scarce cynical to assume they had been drinking; nor, so much being granted, can it be thought exorbitant to suppose them possibly in fault for the squabble that took place. A squabble, I say; but I am willing to call it a riot. And this was the new fault of Laupepa; this it is that was described by a German commodore as "the trampling upon by Malietoa of the German Emperor." I pass the rhetoric by to examine the point of liability. Four natives were brought to trial for this horrid fact: not before a native judge, but before the German magistrate of the tripartite municipality of Apia. One was acquitted, one condemned for theft, and two for assault. On appeal, not to Malietoa, but to the three consuls, the case was by a majority of two to one returned to the magistrate and (as far as I can learn) was then allowed to drop. Consul Becker himself laid the chief blame on one of the policemen of the municipality, a half-white of the name of Scanlon. Him he sought to have discharged, but was again baffled by his brother consuls. Where, in all this, are we to find a corner of responsibility for the king of Samoa? Scanlon, the alleged author of the outrage, was a half-white; as Becker was to learn to his cost, he claimed to be an American subject; and he was not even in the king's employment. Apia, the scene of the outrage, was outside the king's jurisdiction by treaty; by the choice of Germany, he was not so much as allowed to fly his flag there. And the denial of justice (if justice were denied) rested with the consuls of Britain and the

States.

But when a dog is to be beaten, any stick will serve. In the meanwhile, on the proposition of Mr. Bayard, the Washington conference on Samoan affairs was adjourned till autumn, so that "the ministers of Germany and Great Britain might submit the protocols to their respective Governments." "You propose that the conference is to adjourn and not to be broken up?" asked Sir Lionel West. "To adjourn for the reasons stated," replied Bayard. This was on July 26th; and, twenty-nine days later, by Wednesday the 24th of August, Germany had practically seized Samoa. For this flagrant breach of faith one excuse is openly alleged; another whispered. It is openly alleged that Bayard had shown himself impracticable; it is whispered that the Hawaiian embassy was an expression of American intrigue, and that the Germans only did as they were done by. The sufficiency of these excuses may be left to the discretion of the reader. But, however excused, the breach of faith was public and express; it must have been deliberately predetermined and it was resented in the States as a deliberate insult.

By the middle of August 1887 there were five sail of German war-ships in Apia bay: the Bismarck, of 3000 tons displacement; the Carola, the Sophie, and the Olga, all considerable ships; and the beautiful Adler, which lies there to this day, kanted on her beam, dismantled, scarlet with rust, the day showing through her ribs. They waited inactive, as a burglar waits till the patrol goes by. And on the 23rd, when the mail had left for Sydney, when the eyes of the world were withdrawn, and Samoa plunged again for a period of weeks into her original island-obscurity, Becker opened his guns. The policy was too cunning to seem dignified; it gave to conduct which would otherwise have seemed bold and even brutally straightforward, the appearance of a timid ambuscade; and helped to shake men's reliance on the word of Germany. On the day named, an ultimatum reached Malietoa at Afenga, whither he had retired months before to avoid friction. A fine of one thousand dollars and an ifo, or public humiliation, were demanded for the affair of the Emperor's birthday. Twelve thousand dollars were to be "paid quickly" for thefts from German plantations in the course of the last four years. "It is my opinion that there is nothing just or correct in Samoa while you are at the head of the government," concluded Becker. "I shall be at Afenga in the morning of to-morrow, Wednesday, at 11 A.M." The blow fell on Laupepa (in his own expression) "out of the bush"; the dilatory fellow had seen things hang over so long, he had perhaps begun to suppose they might hang over for ever; and here was ruin at the door. He rode at once to Apia, and summoned his chiefs. The council lasted all night long. Many voices were for defiance. But Laupepa had grown inured to a policy of procrastination; and the answer ultimately drawn only begged for delay till Saturday, the 27th. So soon as it was signed, the king took horse and fled in the early morning to Afenga; the council hastily dispersed; and only three chiefs, Selu, Seumanu, and Le Māmea, remained by the government building, tremulously expectant of the result.

By seven the letter was received. By 7.30 Becker arrived in person, inquired for Laupepa, was evasively answered, and declared war on the spot. Before eight, the Germans (seven hundred men and six guns) came ashore and seized and hoisted German colours on the government building. The three chiefs had made good haste to escape; but a considerable booty was made of government papers, fire-arms, and some seventeen thousand cartridges. Then followed a scene which long rankled in the minds of the white inhabitants, when the German marines raided the town in search of Malietoa, burst into private houses, and were accused (I am willing to believe on slender grounds) of violence to private persons.

On the morrow, the 25th, one of the German war-ships, which had been despatched to Leulumoenga over night re-entered the bay, flying the Tamasese colours at the fore. The new king was given a royal salute of twenty-one guns, marched through the town by the commodore and a German guard of honour, and established on Mulinuu with two or three hundred warriors. Becker announced his recognition to the other consuls. These replied by proclaiming Malietoa, and in the usual mealy-mouthed manner advised Samoans to do nothing. On the 27th martial law was declared; and on the 1st September the German squadron dispersed about the group, bearing along with them the proclamations of the new king. Tamasese was now a great man, to have five iron war-ships for his post-runners. But the moment was critical. The revolution had to be explained, the chiefs persuaded to assemble at a fono summoned for the 15th; and the ships carried not only a store of printed documents, but a squad of Tamasese orators upon their round.

Such was the German coup d'état. They had declared war with a squadron of five ships upon a single man; that man, late king of the group, was in hiding on the mountains; and their own nominee, backed by German guns and bayonets, sat in his stead in Mulinuu.

One of the first acts of Malietoa, on fleeing to the bush, was to send for Mataafa twice: "I am alone in the bush; if you do not come quickly you will find me bound." It is to be understood the men were near kinsmen, and had (if they had nothing else) a common jealousy. At the urgent cry, Mataafa set forth from Falefá, and came to Mulinuu to Tamasese. "What is this that you and the German commodore have decided on doing?" he inquired. "I am going to obey the German consul," replied Tamasese, "whose wish it is that I should be the king and that all Samoa should assemble here." "Do not pursue in wrath against Malietoa," said Mataafa "but try to bring about a compromise, and form a united government." "Very well," said Tamasese, "leave it to me, and I will try." From Mulinuu, Mataafa went on board the Bismarck, and was graciously received. "Probably," said the commodore, "we shall bring about a reconciliation of all Samoa through you"; and then asked his visitor if he bore any affection to Malietoa. "Yes," said Mataafa. "And to Tamasese?" "To him also; and if you desire the weal of Samoa, you will allow either him or me to bring about a reconciliation." "If it were my will," said the commodore, "I would do as you say. But I have no will in the matter. I have instructions from the Kaiser, and I cannot go back again from what I have been sent to do." "I thought you would be commanded," said Mataafa, "if you brought about the weal of Samoa." "I will tell you," said the commodore. "All shall go quietly. But there is one thing that must be done: Malietoa must be deposed. I will do nothing to him beyond; he will only be kept on board for a couple of months and be well treated, just as we Germans did to the French chief [Napoleon III.] some time ago, whom we kept a while and cared for well." Becker was no less explicit: war, he told Sewall, should not cease till the Germans had custody of Malietoa and Tamasese should be recognised.

Meantime, in the Malietoa provinces, a profound impression was received. People trooped to their fugitive sovereign in the bush. Many natives in Apia brought their treasures, and stored them in the houses of white friends. The Tamasese orators were sometimes ill received. Over in Savaii, they found the village of Satupaitea deserted, save for a few lads at cricket. These they harangued, and were rewarded with ironical applause; and the proclamation, as soon as they had departed, was torn down. For this offence the village was ultimately burned by German sailors, in a very decent and orderly style, on the 3rd September. This was the dinner-bell of the fono on the 15th. The threat conveyed in the terms of the summons—"If any government district does not quickly obey this direction, I will make war on that government district"—was thus commented on and reinforced. And the meeting was in consequence well attended by chiefs of all parties. They found themselves unarmed among the armed warriors of Tamasese and the marines of the German squadron, and under the guns of five strong ships. Brandeis rose; it was his first open appearance, the German firm signing its revolutionary work. His words were few and uncompromising: "Great are my thanks that the chiefs and heads of families of the whole of Samoa are assembled here this day. It is strictly forbidden that any discussion should take place as to whether it is good or not that Tamasese is king of Samoa, whether at this fono or at any future fono. I place for your signature the following: 'We inform all the people of Samoa of what follows: (1) The government of Samoa has been assumed by King Tuiaana Tamasese. (2) By order of the king, it was directed that a fono should take place to-day, composed of the chiefs and heads of families, and we have obeyed the summons. We have signed our names under this, 15th September 1887." Needs must under all these guns; and the paper was signed, but not without open sullenness. The bearing of Mataafa in particular was long remembered against him by the Germans. "Do you not see the king?" said the commodore reprovingly. "His father was no king," was the bold answer. A bolder still has been printed, but this is Mataafa's own recollection of the passage. On the next day, the chiefs were all ordered back to shake hands with Tamasese. Again they obeyed; but again their attitude was menacing, and some, it is said, audibly murmured as they gave their hands.

It is time to follow the poor Sheet of Paper (literal meaning of Laupepa), who was now to be blown so broadly over the face of earth. As soon as news reached him of the declaration of war, he fled from Afenga to Tanungamanono, a hamlet in the bush, about a mile and a half behind Apia, where he lurked some days. On the 24th, Selu, his secretary, despatched to the American consul an anxious appeal, his majesty's "cry and prayer" in behalf of "this weak people." By August 30th, the Germans had word of his lurking-place, surrounded the hamlet under cloud of night, and in the early morning burst with a force of sailors on the houses. The people fled on all sides, and were fired upon. One boy was shot in the hand, the first blood of the war. But the king was nowhere to be found; he had wandered farther, over the woody mountains, the backbone of the land, towards Siumu and Safata. Here, in a safe place, he built himself a town in the forest, where he received a continual stream of visitors and messengers. Day after day the German blue-jackets were employed in the hopeless enterprise of beating the forests for the fugitive; day after day they were suffered to pass unhurt under the guns of ambushed Samoans; day after day they returned, exhausted and disappointed, to Apia. Seumanu Tafa, high chief of Apia, was known to be in the forest with the king; his wife, Fatuila, was seized, imprisoned in the German hospital, and when it was thought her spirit was sufficiently reduced, brought up for cross-examination. The wise lady confined herself in answer to a single word. "Is your husband near Apia?" "Yes." "Is he far from Apia?" "Yes." "Is he with the king?" "Yes." "Are he and the king in different places?" "Yes." Whereupon the witness was discharged. About the 10th of September, Laupepa was secretly in Apia at the American consulate with two companions. The German pickets were close set and visited by a strong patrol; and on his return, his party was observed and hailed and fired on by a sentry. They ran away on all fours in the dark, and so doing plumped upon another sentry, whom Laupepa grappled and flung in a ditch; for the Sheet of Paper, although infirm of character, is, like most Samoans, of an able body. The second sentry (like the first) fired after his assailants at random in the dark; and the two shots awoke the curiosity of Apia. On the afternoon of the 16th, the day of the hand-shakings, Suatele, a high chief, despatched two boys across the island with a letter. They were most of the night upon the road; it was near three in the morning before the sentries in the camp of Malietoa beheld their lantern drawing near out of the wood; but the king was at once awakened. The news was decisive and the letter peremptory; if Malietoa did not give himself up before ten on the morrow, he was told that great sorrows must befall his country. I have not been able to draw Laupepa as a hero; but he is a man of certain virtues, which the Germans had now given him an occasion to display. Without hesitation he sacrificed himself, penned his touching farewell to Samoa, and making more expedition than the messengers, passed early behind Apia to the banks of the Vaisingano. As he passed, he detached a messenger to Mataafa at the Catholic mission. Mataafa followed by the same road, and the pair met at the river-side and went and sat together in a house. All present were in tears. "Do not let us weep," said the talking man, Lauati. "We have no cause for shame. We do not yield to Tamasese, but to the invincible strangers." The departing king bequeathed the care of his country to Mataafa; and when the latter sought to console him with the commodore's promises, he shook his head, and declared his assurance that he was going to a life of exile, and perhaps to death. About two o'clock the meeting broke up; Mataafa returned to the Catholic mission by the back of the town; and Malietoa proceeded by the beach road to the German naval hospital, where he was received (as he owns, with perfect civility) by Brandeis. About three, Becker brought him forth again. As they went to the wharf, the people wept and clung to their departing monarch. A boat carried him on board the Bismarck, and he vanished from his countrymen. Yet it was long rumoured that he still lay in the harbour; and so late as October 7th, a boy, who had been paddling round the Carola, professed to have seen and spoken with him. Here again the needless mystery affected by the Germans bitterly disserved them. The uncertainty which thus hung over Laupepa's fate, kept his name continually in men's mouths. The words of his farewell rang in their ears: "To all Samoa: On account of my great love to my country and my great affection to all Samoa, this is the reason that I deliver up my body to the German government. That government may do as they wish to me. The reason of this is, because I do not desire that the blood of Samoa shall be spilt for me again. But I do not know what is my offence which has caused their anger to me and to my country." And then, apostrophising the different provinces: "Tuamasanga, farewell! Manono and family, farewell! So, also, Salafai, Tutuila, Aana, and Atua, farewell! If we do not again see one another in this world, pray that we may be again together above." So the sheep departed with the halo of a saint, and men thought of him as of some King Arthur snatched into Avilion.

On board the Bismarck, the commodore shook hands with him, told him he was to be "taken away from all the chiefs with whom he had been accustomed," and had him taken to the wardroom under guard. The next day he was sent to sea in the Adler. There went with him his brother Moli, one Meisake, and one Alualu, half-caste German, to interpret. He was respectfully used; he dined in the stern with the officers, but the boys dined "near where the fire was." They come to a "newly-formed place" in Australia, where the Albatross was lying, and a British ship, which he knew to be a man-of-war "because the officers were nicely dressed and wore epaulettes." Here he was transhipped, "in a boat with a screen," which he supposed was to conceal him from the British ship; and on board the Albatross was sent below and told he must stay there till they had sailed. Later, however, he was allowed to come on deck, where he found they had rigged a screen (perhaps an awning) under which he walked, looking at "the newly-formed settlement," and admiring a big house "where he was sure the governor lived." From Australia, they sailed some time, and reached an anchorage where a consul-general came on board, and where Laupepa was only allowed on deck at night. He could then see the lights of a town with wharves; he supposes Cape Town. Off the Cameroons they anchored or lay-to, far at sea, and sent a boat ashore to see (he supposes) that there was no British man-of-war. It was the next morning before the boat returned, when the Albatross stood in and came to anchor near another German ship. Here Alualu came to him on deck and told him this was the place. "That is an astonishing thing," said he. "I thought I was to go to Germany, I do not know what this means; I do not know what will be the end of it; my heart is troubled." Whereupon Alualu burst into tears. A little after, Laupepa was called below to the captain and the governor. The last addressed him: "This is my own place, a good place, a warm place. My house is not yet finished, but when it is, you shall live in one of my rooms until I can make a house for you." Then he was taken ashore and brought to a tall, iron house. "This house is regulated," said the governor; "there is no fire allowed to burn in it." In one part of this house, weapons of the government were hung up; there was a passage, and on the other side of the passage, fifty criminals were chained together, two and two, by the ankles. The windows were out of reach; and there was only one door, which was opened at six in the morning and shut again at six at night. All day he had his liberty, went to the Baptist Mission, and walked about viewing the negroes, who were "like the sand on the seashore" for number. At six they were called into the house and shut in for the night without beds or lights. "Although they gave me no light," said he, with a smile, "I could see I was in a prison." Good food was given him: biscuits, "tea made with warm water," beef, etc.; all excellent. Once, in their walks, they spied a breadfruit tree bearing in the garden of an English merchant, ran back to the prison to get a shilling, and came and offered to purchase. "I am not going to sell breadfruit to you people," said the merchant; "come and take what you like." Here Malietoa interrupted himself to say it was the only tree bearing in the Cameroons. "The governor had none, or he would have given it to me." On the passage from the Cameroons to Germany, he had great delight to see the cliffs of England. He saw "the rocks shining in the sun, and three hours later was surprised to find them sunk in the heavens." He saw also wharves and immense buildings; perhaps Dover and its castle. In Hamburg, after breakfast, Mr. Weber, who had now finally "ceased from troubling" Samoa, came on board, and carried him ashore "suitably" in a steam launch to "a large house of the government," where he stayed till noon. At noon Weber told him he was going to "the place where ships are anchored that go to Samoa," and led him to "a very magnificent house, with carriages inside and a wonderful roof of glass"; to wit, the railway station. They were benighted on the train, and then went in "something with a house, drawn by horses, which had windows and many decks"; plainly an omnibus. Here (at Bremen or Bremerhaven, I believe) they stayed some while in "a house of five hundred rooms"; then were got on board the Nürnberg (as they understood) for Samoa, anchored in England on a Sunday, were joined en route by the famous Dr. Knappe, passed through "a narrow passage where they went very slow and which was just like a river," and beheld with exhilarated curiosity that Red Sea of which they had learned so much in their Bibles. At last, "at the hour when the fires burn red," they came to a place where was a German man-of-war. Laupepa was called, with one of the boys, on deck, when he found a German officer awaiting him, and a steam launch alongside, and was told he must now leave his brother and go elsewhere. "I cannot go like this," he cried. "You must let me see my brother and the other old men"—a term of courtesy. Knappe, who seems always to have been good-natured, revised his orders, and consented not only to an interview, but to allow Moli to continue to accompany the king. So these two were carried to the man-of-war, and sailed many a day, still supposing themselves bound for Samoa; and lo! she came to a country the like of which they had never dreamed of, and cast anchor in the great lagoon of Jaluit; and upon that narrow land the exiles were set on shore. This was the part of his captivity on which he looked back with the most bitterness. It was the last, for one thing, and he was worn down with the long suspense, and terror, and deception. He could not bear the brackish water; and though "the Germans were still good to him, and gave him beef and biscuit and tea," he suffered from the lack of vegetable food.

Such is the narrative of this simple exile. I have not sought to correct it by extraneous testimony. It is not so much the facts that are historical, as the man's attitude. No one could hear this tale as he originally told it in my hearing—I think none can read it as here condensed and unadorned—without admiring the fairness and simplicity of the Samoan; and wondering at the want of heart—or want of humour—in so many successive civilised Germans, that they should have continued to surround this infant with the secrecy of state.

CHAPTER IV—BRANDEIS

September '87 to August '88

So Tamasese was on the throne, and Brandeis behind it; and I have now to deal with their brief and luckless reign. That it was the reign of Brandeis needs not to be argued: the policy is throughout that of an able, over-hasty white, with eyes and ideas. But it should be borne in mind that he had a double task, and must first lead his sovereign, before he could begin to drive their common subjects. Meanwhile, he himself was exposed (if all tales be true) to much dictation and interference, and to some "cumbrous aid," from the consulate and the firm. And to one of these aids, the suppression of the municipality, I am inclined to attribute his ultimate failure.

The white enemies of the new regimen were of two classes. In the first stood Moors and the employés of MacArthur, the two chief rivals of the firm, who saw with jealousy a clerk (or a so-called clerk) of their competitors advanced to the chief power. The second class, that of the officials, numbered at first exactly one. Wilson, the English acting consul, is understood to have held strict orders to help Germany. Commander Leary, of the Adams, the American captain, when he arrived, on the 16th October, and for some time after, seemed devoted to the German interest, and spent his days with a German officer, Captain Von Widersheim, who was deservedly beloved by all who knew him. There remains the American consul-general, Harold Marsh Sewall, a young man of high spirit and a generous disposition. He had obeyed the orders of his government with a grudge; and looked back on his past action with regret almost to be called repentance. From the moment of the declaration of war against Laupepa, we find him standing forth in bold, consistent, and sometimes rather captious opposition, stirring up his government at home with clear and forcible despatches, and on the spot grasping at every opportunity to thrust a stick into the German wheels. For some while, he and Moors fought their difficult battle in conjunction; in the course of which, first one, and then the other, paid a visit home to reason with the authorities at Washington; and during the consul's absence, there was found an American clerk in Apia, William Blacklock, to perform the duties of the office with remarkable ability and courage. The three names just brought together, Sewall, Moors, and Blacklock, make the head and front of the opposition; if Tamasese fell, if Brandeis was driven forth, if the treaty of Berlin was signed, theirs is the blame or the credit.

To understand the feelings of self-reproach and bitterness with which Sewall took the field, the reader must see Laupepa's letter of farewell to the consuls of England and America. It is singular that this far from brilliant or dignified monarch, writing in the forest, in heaviness of spirit and under pressure for time, should have left behind him not only one, but two remarkable and most effective documents. The farewell to his people was touching; the farewell to the consuls, for a man of the character of Sewall, must have cut like a whip. "When the chief Tamasese and others first moved the present troubles," he wrote, "it was my wish to punish them and put an end to the rebellion; but I yielded to the advice of the British and American consuls. Assistance and protection was repeatedly promised to me and my government, if I abstained from bringing war upon my country. Relying upon these promises, I did not put down the rebellion. Now I find that war has been made upon me by the Emperor of Germany, and Tamasese has been proclaimed king of Samoa. I desire to remind you of the promises so frequently made by your government, and trust that you will so far redeem them as to cause the lives and liberties of my chiefs and people to be respected."

Sewall's immediate adversary was, of course, Becker. I have formed an opinion of this gentleman, largely from his printed despatches, which I am at a loss to put in words. Astute, ingenious, capable, at moments almost witty with a kind of glacial wit in action, he displayed in the course of this affair every description of capacity but that which is alone useful and which springs from a knowledge of men's natures. It chanced that one of Sewall's early moves played into his hands, and he was swift to seize and to improve the advantage. The neutral territory and the tripartite municipality of Apia were eyesores to the German consulate and Brandeis. By landing Tamasese's two or three hundred warriors at Mulinuu, as Becker himself owns, they had

51

infringed the treaties, and Sewall entered protest twice. There were two ways of escaping this dilemma: one was to withdraw the warriors; the other, by some hocus-pocus, to abrogate the neutrality. And the second had subsidiary advantages: it would restore the taxes of the richest district in the islands to the Samoan king; and it would enable them to substitute over the royal seat the flag of Germany for the new flag of Tamasese. It is true (and it was the subject of much remark) that these two could hardly be distinguished by the naked eye; but their effects were different. To seat the puppet king on German land and under German colours, so that any rebellion was constructive war on Germany, was a trick apparently invented by Becker, and which we shall find was repeated and persevered in till the end.

Otto Martin was at this time magistrate in the municipality. The post was held in turn by the three nationalities; Martin had served far beyond his term, and should have been succeeded months before by an American. To make the change it was necessary to hold a meeting of the municipal board, consisting of the three consuls, each backed by an assessor. And for some time these meetings had been evaded or refused by the German consul. As long as it was agreed to continue Martin, Becker had attended regularly; as soon as Sewall indicated a wish for his removal, Becker tacitly suspended the municipality by refusing to appear. This policy was now the more necessary; for if the whole existence of the municipality were a check on the freedom of the new government, it was plainly less so when the power to enforce and punish lay in German hands. For some while back the Malietoa flag had been flown on the municipal building: Becker denies this; I am sorry; my information obliges me to suppose he is in error. Sewall, with post-mortem loyalty to the past, insisted that this flag should be continued. And Becker immediately made his point. He declared, justly enough, that the proposal was hostile, and argued that it was impossible he should attend a meeting under a flag with which his sovereign was at war. Upon one occasion of urgency, he was invited to meet the two other consuls at the British consulate; even this he refused; and for four months the municipality slumbered, Martin still in office. In the month of October, in consequence, the British and American ratepayers announced they would refuse to pay. Becker doubtless rubbed his hands. On Saturday, the 10th, the chief Tamaseu, a Malietoa man of substance and good character, was arrested on a charge of theft believed to be vexatious, and cast by Martin into the municipal prison. He sent to Moors, who was his tenant and owed him money at the time, for bail. Moors applied to Sewall, ranking consul. After some search, Martin was found and refused to consider bail before the Monday morning. Whereupon Sewall demanded the keys from the gaoler, accepted Moors's verbal recognisances, and set Tamaseu free.

Things were now at a deadlock; and Becker astonished every one by agreeing to a meeting on the 14th. It seems he knew what to expect. Writing on the 13th at least, he prophesies that the meeting will be held in vain, that the municipality must lapse, and the government of Tamasese step in. On the 14th, Sewall left his consulate in time, and walked some part of the way to the place of meeting in company with Wilson, the English pro-consul. But he had forgotten a paper, and in an evil hour returned for it alone. Wilson arrived without him, and Becker broke up the meeting for want of a quorum. There was some unedifying disputation as to whether he had waited ten or twenty minutes, whether he had been officially or unofficially informed by Wilson that Sewall was on the way, whether the statement had been made to himself or to Weber {1} in answer to a question, and whether he had heard Wilson's answer or only Weber's question: all otiose; if he heard the question, he was bound to have waited for the answer; if he heard it not, he should have put it himself; and it was the manifest truth that he rejoiced in his occasion. "Sir," he wrote to Sewall, "I have the honour to inform you that, to my regret, I am obliged to consider the municipal government to be provisionally in abeyance since you have withdrawn your consent to the continuation of Mr. Martin in his position as magistrate, and since you have refused to take part in the meeting of the municipal board agreed to for the purpose of electing a magistrate. The government of the town and district of the municipality rests, as long as the municipality is in abeyance, with the Samoan government. The Samoan government has taken over the administration, and has applied to the commander of the imperial German squadron for assistance in the preservation of good order." This letter was not delivered until 4 P.M. By three, sailors had been landed. Already German colours flew over Tamasese's headquarters at Mulinuu, and German guards had occupied the hospital, the German consulate, and the municipal gaol and court-house, where they stood to arms under the flag of Tamasese. The same day Sewall wrote to protest. Receiving no reply, he issued on the morrow a proclamation bidding all Americans look to himself alone. On the 26th, he wrote again to Becker, and on the 27th received this genial reply: "Sir, your high favour of the 26th of this month, I give myself the honour of acknowledging. At the same time I acknowledge the receipt of your high favour of the 14th October in reply to my communication of the same date, which contained the information of the suspension of the arrangements for the municipal government." There the correspondence ceased. And on the 18th January came the last step of this irritating intrigue when Tamasese appointed a judge—and the judge proved to be Martin.

Thus was the adventure of the Castle Municipal achieved by Sir Becker the chivalrous. The taxes of Apia, the gaol, the police, all passed into the hands of Tamasese-Brandeis; a German was secured upon the bench; and the German flag might wave over her puppet unquestioned. But there is a law of human nature which diplomatists should be taught at school, and it seems they are not; that men can tolerate bare injustice, but not the combination of injustice and subterfuge. Hence the chequered career of the thimble-rigger. Had the municipality been seized by open force, there might have been complaint, it would not have aroused the same lasting grudge.

This grudge was an ill gift to bring to Brandeis, who had trouble enough in front of him without. He was an alien, he was supported by the guns of alien war-ships, and he had come to do an alien's work, highly needful for Samoa, but essentially unpopular with all Samoans. The law to be enforced, causes of dispute between white and brown to be eliminated, taxes to be raised, a central power created, the country opened up, the native race taught industry: all these were detestable to the natives, and to all of these he must set his hand. The more I learn of his brief term of rule, the more I learn to admire him, and to wish we had his like.

In the face of bitter native opposition, he got some roads accomplished. He set up beacons. The taxes he enforced with necessary vigour. By the 6th of January, Aua and Fangatonga, districts in Tutuila, having made a difficulty, Brandeis is down at the island in a schooner, with the Adler at his heels, seizes the chief Maunga, fines the recalcitrant districts in three hundred dollars for expenses, and orders all to be in by April 20th, which if it is not, "not one thing will be done," he proclaimed, "but war declared against you, and the principal chiefs taken to a distant island." He forbade mortgages of copra, a frequent source of trickery and quarrel; and to clear off those already contracted, passed a severe but salutary law. Each individual or family was first to pay off its own obligation; that settled, the free man was to pay for the indebted village, the free village for the indebted province, and one island for another. Samoa, he declared, should be free of debt within a year. Had he given it three years, and gone more gently, I believe it might have been accomplished. To make it the more possible, he sought to interdict the natives from buying cotton stuffs and to oblige them to dress (at least for the time) in their own tapa. He laid the beginnings of a royal territorial army. The first draft was in his hands drilling. But it was not so much on drill that he depended; it was his hope to kindle in these men an esprit de corps, which should weaken the old local jealousies and bonds, and found a central or national party in the islands. Looking far before, and with a wisdom beyond that of many merchants, he had condemned the single dependence placed on copra for the national livelihood. His recruits, even as they drilled, were taught to plant cacao. Each, his term of active service finished, should return to his own land and plant and cultivate a stipulated area. Thus, as the young men continued to pass through the army, habits of discipline and industry, a central sentiment, the principles of the new culture, and actual gardens of cacao, should be concurrently spread over the face of the islands.

Tamasese received, including his household expenses, 1960 dollars a year; Brandeis, 2400. All such disproportions are regrettable, but this is not extreme: we have seen horses of a different colour since then. And the Tamaseseites, with true Samoan ostentation, offered to increase the salary of their white premier: an offer he had the wisdom and good feeling to refuse. A European chief of police received twelve hundred. There were eight head judges, one to each province, and appeal lay from the district judge to the provincial, thence to Mulinuu. From all salaries (I gather) a small monthly guarantee was withheld. The army was to cost from three to four thousand, Apia (many whites refusing to pay taxes since the suppression of the municipality) might cost three thousand more: Sir Becker's high feat of arms coming expensive (it will be noticed) even in money. The whole outlay was estimated at twenty-seven thousand; and the revenue forty thousand: a sum Samoa is well able to pay.

Such were the arrangements and some of the ideas of this strong, ardent, and sanguine man. Of criticisms upon his conduct, beyond the general consent that he was rather harsh and in too great a hurry, few are articulate. The native paper of complaints was particularly childish. Out of twenty-three counts, the first two refer to the private character of Brandeis and Tamasese. Three complain that Samoan officials were kept in the dark as to the finances; one, of the tapa law; one, of the direct appointment of chiefs by Tamasese-Brandeis, the sort of mistake into which Europeans in the South Seas fall so readily; one, of the enforced labour of chiefs; one, of the taxes; and one, of the roads. This I may give in full from the very lame translation in the American white book. "The roads that were made were called the Government Roads; they were six fathoms wide. Their making caused much damage to Samoa's lands and what was planted on it. The Samoans cried on account of their lands, which were taken high-handedly and abused. They again cried on account of the loss of what they had planted, which was now thrown away in a high-handed way, without any regard being shown or question asked of the owner of the land, or any compensation offered for the damage done. This was different with foreigners' land; in their case permission was first asked to make the roads; the foreigners were paid for any destruction made." The sting of this count was, I fancy, in the last clause. No less than six articles complain of the administration of the law; and I believe that was never satisfactory. Brandeis told me himself he was never yet satisfied with any native judge. And men say (and it seems to fit in well with his hasty and eager character) that he would legislate by word of mouth; sometimes forget what he had said; and, on the same question arising in another province, decide it perhaps otherwise. I gather, on the whole, our artillery captain was not great in law. Two articles refer to a matter I must deal with more at length, and rather from the point of view of the white residents.

The common charge against Brandeis was that of favouring the German firm. Coming as he did, this was inevitable. Weber had bought Steinberger with hard cash; that was matter of history. The present government he did not even require to buy, having founded it by his intrigues, and introduced the premier to Samoa through the doors of his own office. And the effect of the initial blunder was kept alive by the chatter of the clerks in bar-rooms, boasting themselves of the new government and prophesying annihilation to all rivals. The time of raising a tax is the harvest of the merchants; it is the time when copra will be made, and must be sold; and the intention of the German firm, first in the time of Steinberger, and again in April and May, 1888, with Brandeis, was to seize and handle the whole operation. Their chief rivals were the Messrs. MacArthur; and it seems beyond question that provincial governors more than once issued orders forbidding Samoans to take money from "the New Zealand firm." These, when they were brought to his notice, Brandeis disowned, and he is entitled to be heard. No man can live long in Samoa and not have his honesty impugned. But the accusations against Brandeis's veracity are both few and obscure. I believe he was as straight as his sword. The governors doubtless issued these orders, but there were plenty besides Brandeis to suggest them. Every wandering clerk from the firm's office, every plantation manager, would be dinning the same story in the native ear. And here again the initial blunder hung about the neck of Brandeis, a ton's weight. The natives, as well as the whites, had seen their premier masquerading on a stool in the office; in the eyes of the natives, as well as in those of the whites, he must always have retained the mark of servitude from that ill-judged passage; and they would be inclined to look behind and above him, to the great house of Misi Ueba. The government was like a vista of puppets. People did not trouble with Tamasese, if they got speech with Brandeis; in the same way, they might not always trouble to ask Brandeis, if they had a hint direct from Misi Ueba. In only one case, though it seems to have had many developments, do I find the premier personally committed. The MacArthurs claimed the copra of Fasitotai on a district mortgage of three hundred dollars. The German firm accepted a mortgage of the whole province of Aana, claimed the copra of Fasitotai as that of a part of Aana, and were supported by the government. Here Brandeis was false to his own principle, that personal and village debts should come before provincial.

But the case occurred before the promulgation of the law, and was, as a matter of fact, the cause of it; so the most we can say is that he changed his mind, and changed it for the better. If the history of his government be considered—how it originated in an intrigue between the firm and the consulate, and was (for the firm's sake alone) supported by the consulate with foreign bayonets—the existence of the least doubt on the man's action must seem marvellous. We should have looked to find him playing openly and wholly into their hands; that he did not, implies great independence and much secret friction; and I believe (if the truth were known) the firm would be found to have been disgusted with the stubbornness of its intended tool, and Brandeis often impatient of the demands of his creators.

But I may seem to exaggerate the degree of white opposition. And it is true that before fate overtook the Brandeis government, it appeared to enjoy the fruits of victory in Apia; and one dissident, the unconquerable Moors, stood out alone to refuse his taxes. But the victory was in appearance only; the opposition was latent; it found vent in talk, and thus reacted on the natives; upon the least excuse, it was ready to flame forth again. And this is the more singular because some were far from out of sympathy with the native policy pursued. When I met Captain Brandeis, he was amazed at my attitude. "Whom did you find in Apia to tell you so much good of me?" he asked. I named one of my informants. "He?" he cried. "If he thought all that, why did he not help me?" I told him as well as I was able. The man was a merchant. He beheld in the government of Brandeis a government created by and for the firm who were his rivals. If Brandeis were minded to deal fairly, where was the probability that he would be allowed? If Brandeis insisted and were strong enough to prevail, what guarantee that, as soon as the government were fairly accepted, Brandeis might not be removed? Here was the attitude of the hour; and I am glad to find it clearly set forth in a despatch of Sewall's, June 18th, 1888, when he commends the law against mortgages, and goes on: "Whether the author of this law will carry out the good intentions which he professes—whether he will be allowed to do so, if he desires, against the opposition of those who placed him in power and protect him in the possession of it—may well be doubted." Brandeis had come to Apia in the firm's livery. Even while he promised neutrality in commerce, the clerks were prating a different story in the bar-rooms; and the late high feat of the knight-errant, Becker, had killed all confidence in Germans at the root. By these three impolicies, the German adventure in Samoa was defeated.

I imply that the handful of whites were the true obstacle, not the thousands of malcontent Samoans; for had the whites frankly accepted Brandeis, the path of Germany was clear, and the end of their policy, however troublesome might be its course, was obvious. But this is not to say that the natives were content. In a sense, indeed, their opposition was continuous. There will always be opposition in Samoa when taxes are imposed; and the deportation of Malietoa stuck in men's throats. Tuiatua Mataafa refused to act under the new government from the beginning, and Tamasese usurped his place and title. As early as February, I find him signing himself "Tuiaana Tuiatua Tamasese," the first step on a dangerous path. Asi, like Mataafa, disclaimed his chiefship and declared himself a private person; but he was more rudely dealt with. German sailors surrounded his house in the night, burst in, and dragged the women out of the mosquito nets—an offence against Samoan manners. No Asi was to be found; but at last they were shown his fishing-lights on the reef, rowed out, took him as he was, and carried him on board a man-of-war, where he was detained some while between-decks. At last, January 16th, after a farewell interview over the ship's side with his wife, he was discharged into a ketch, and along with two other chiefs, Maunga and Tuiletu-funga, deported to the Marshalls. The blow struck fear upon all sides. Le Mámea (a very able chief) was secretly among the malcontents. His family and followers murmured at his weakness; but he continued, throughout the duration of the government, to serve Brandeis with trembling. A circus coming to Apia, he seized at the pretext for escape, and asked leave to accept an engagement in the company. "I will not allow you to make a monkey of yourself," said Brandeis; and the phrase had a success throughout the islands, pungent expressions being so much admired by the natives that they cannot refrain from repeating them, even when they have been levelled at themselves. The assumption of the Atua name spread discontent in that province; many chiefs from thence were convicted of disaffection, and condemned to labour with their hands upon the roads—a great shock to the Samoan sense of the becoming, which was rendered the more sensible by the death of one of the number at his task. Mataafa was involved in the same trouble. His disaffected speech at a meeting of Atua chiefs was betrayed by the girls that made the kava, and the man of the future was called to Apia on safe-conduct, but, after an interview, suffered to return to his lair. The peculiarly tender treatment of Mataafa must be explained by his relationship to Tamasese. Laupepa was of Malietoa blood. The hereditary retainers of the Tupua would see him exiled even with some complacency. But Mataafa was Tupua himself; and Tupua men would probably have murmured, and would perhaps have mutinied, had he been harshly dealt with.

The native opposition, I say, was in a sense continuous. And it kept continuously growing. The sphere of Brandeis was limited to Mulinuu and the north central quarters of Upolu—practically what is shown upon the map opposite. There the taxes were expanded; in the out-districts, men paid their money and saw no return. Here the eye and hand of the dictator were ready to correct the scales of justice; in the out-districts, all things lay at the mercy of the native magistrates, and their oppressions increased with the course of time and the experience of impunity. In the spring of the year, a very intelligent observer had occasion to visit many places in the island of Savaii. "Our lives are not worth living," was the burthen of the popular complaint. "We are groaning under the oppression of these men. We would rather die than continue to endure it." On his return to Apia, he made haste to communicate his impressions to Brandeis. Brandeis replied in an epigram: "Where there has been anarchy in a country, there must be oppression for a time." But unfortunately the terms of the epigram may be reversed; and personal supervision would have been more in season than wit. The same observer who conveyed to him this warning thinks that, if Brandeis had himself visited the districts and inquired into complaints, the blow might yet have been averted and the government saved. At last, upon a certain unconstitutional act of Tamasese, the discontent took life and fire. The act was of his own conception; the dull dog was ambitious. Brandeis declares he would not be dissuaded; perhaps his adviser did not seriously try, perhaps did not dream that in that welter of contradictions, the Samoan constitution, any one point would be considered sacred. I have told how Tamasese assumed the title of Tuiatua. In August 1888 a year after his installation, he took a more formidable step and assumed that of Malietoa. This name, as I have said, is of peculiar honour; it had been given to, it had never been taken from, the exiled Laupepa; those in whose grant it lay, stood punctilious upon their rights; and Tamasese, as the representative of their natural opponents, the Tupua line, was the last who should have had it. And there was yet more, though I almost despair to make it thinkable by Europeans. Certain old mats are handed down, and set huge store by; they may be compared to coats of arms or heirlooms among ourselves; and to the horror of more than one-half of Samoa, Tamasese, the head of the Tupua, began collecting Malietoa mats. It was felt that the cup was full, and men began to prepare secretly for rebellion. The history of the month of August is unknown to whites; it passed altogether in the covert of the woods or in the stealthy councils of Samoans. One ominous sign was to be noted; arms and ammunition began to be purchased or inquired about; and the more wary traders ordered fresh consignments of material of war. But the rest was silence; the government slept in security; and Brandeis was summoned at last from a public dinner, to find rebellion organised, the woods behind Apia full of insurgents, and a plan prepared, and in the very article of execution, to surprise and seize Mulinuu. The timely discovery averted all; and the leaders hastily withdrew towards the south side of the island, leaving in the bush a rear-guard under a young man of the name of Saifaleupolu. According to some accounts, it scarce numbered forty; the leader was no great chief, but a handsome, industrious lad who seems to have been much beloved. And upon this obstacle Brandeis fell. It is the man's fault to be too impatient of results; his public intention to free Samoa of all debt within the year, depicts him; and instead of continuing to temporise and let his enemies weary and disperse, he judged it politic to strike a blow. He struck it, with what seemed to be success, and the sound of it roused Samoa to rebellion.

About two in the morning of August 31st, Apia was wakened by men marching. Day came, and Brandeis and his war-party were already long disappeared in the woods. All morning belated Tamaseseites were still to be seen running with their guns. All morning shots were listened for in vain; but over the top of the forest, far up the mountain, smoke was for some time observed to hang. About ten a dead man was carried in, lashed under a pole like a dead pig, his rosary (for he was a Catholic) hanging nearly to the ground. Next came a young fellow wounded, sitting in a rope swung from a pole; two fellows bearing him, two running behind for a relief. At last about eleven, three or four heavy volleys and a great shouting were heard from the bush town Tanungamanono; the affair was over, the victorious force, on the march back, was there celebrating its victory by the way. Presently after, it marched through Apia, five or six hundred strong, in tolerable order and strutting with the ludicrous assumption of the triumphant islander. Women who had been buying bread ran and gave them loaves. At the tail end came Brandeis himself, smoking a cigar, deadly pale, and with perhaps an increase of his usual nervous manner. One spoke to him by the way. He expressed his sorrow the action had been forced on him. "Poor people, it's all the worse for them!" he said. "It'll have to be done another way now." And it was supposed by his hearer that he referred to intervention from the German war-ships. He meant, he said, to put a stop to head-hunting; his men had taken two that day, he added, but he had not suffered them to bring them in, and they had been left in Tanungamanono. Thither my informant rode, was attracted by the sound of wailing, and saw in a house the two heads washed and combed, and the sister of one of the dead lamenting in the island fashion and kissing the cold face. Soon after, a small grave was dug, the heads were buried in a beef box, and the pastor read the service. The body of Saifaleupolu himself was recovered unmutilated, brought down from the forest, and buried behind Apia.

The same afternoon, the men of Vaimaunga were ordered to report in Mulinuu, where Tamasese's flag was half-masted for the death of a chief in the skirmish. Vaimaunga is that district of Taumasanga which includes the bay and the foothills behind Apia; and both province and district are strong Malietoa. Not one man, it is said, obeyed the summons. Night came, and the town lay in unusual silence; no one abroad; the blinds down around the native houses, the men within sleeping on their arms; the old women keeping watch in pairs. And in the course of the two following days all Vaimaunga was gone into the bush, the very gaoler setting free his prisoners and joining them in their escape. Hear the words of the chiefs in the 23rd article of their complaint: "Some of the chiefs fled to the bush from fear of being reported, fear of German men-of-war, constantly being accused, etc., and Brandeis commanded that they were to be shot on sight. This act was carried out by Brandeis on the 31st day of August, 1888. After this we evaded these laws; we could not stand them; our patience was worn out with the constant wickedness of Tamasese and Brandeis. We were tired out and could stand no longer the acts of these two men."

So through an ill-timed skirmish, two severed heads, and a dead body, the rule of Brandeis came to a sudden end. We shall see him a while longer fighting for existence in a losing battle; but his government—take it for all in all, the most promising that has ever been in these unlucky islands—was from that hour a piece of history.

CHAPTER V—THE BATTLE OF MATAUTU

September 1888

The revolution had all the character of a popular movement. Many of the high chiefs were detained in Mulinuu; the commons trooped to the bush under inferior leaders. A camp was chosen near Faleula, threatening Mulinuu, well placed for the arrival of recruits and close to a German plantation from which the force could be subsisted. Manono came, all Tuamasanga, much of Savaii, and part of Aana, Tamasese's own government and titular seat. Both sides were arming. It was a brave day for the trader, though not so brave as some that followed, when a single cartridge is said to have been sold for twelve cents currency—between nine and ten cents gold. Yet even among the traders a strong party feeling reigned, and it was the common practice to ask a purchaser upon which side he meant to fight.

On September 5th, Brandeis published a letter: "To the chiefs of Tuamasanga, Manono, and Faasaleleanga in the Bush: Chiefs, by authority of his majesty Tamasese, the king of Samoa, I make known to you all that the German man-of-war is about to go together with a Samoan fleet for the purpose of burning Manono. After this island is all burnt, 'tis good if the people return to Manono and live quiet. To the people of Faasaleleanga I say, return to your houses and stop there. The same to those belonging to Tuamasanga. If you obey this instruction, then you will all be forgiven; if you do not obey, then all your villages will be burnt like Manono. These instructions are made in truth in the sight of God in the Heaven." The same morning, accordingly, the Adler steamed out of the bay with a force of Tamasese warriors and some native boats in tow, the Samoan fleet in question. Manono was shelled; the Tamasese warriors, under the conduct of a Manono traitor, who paid before many days the forfeit of his blood, landed and did some damage, but were driven away by the sight of a force returning from the mainland; no one was hurt, for the women and children, who alone remained on the island, found a refuge in the bush; and the Adler and her acolytes returned the same evening. The letter had been energetic; the performance fell below the programme. The demonstration annoyed and yet re-assured the insurgents, and it fully disclosed to the Germans a new enemy.

Captain Yon Widersheim had been relieved. His successor, Captain Fritze, was an officer of a different stamp. I have nothing to say of him but good; he seems to have obeyed the consul's requisitions with secret distaste; his despatches were of admirable candour; but his habits were retired, he spoke little English, and was far indeed from inheriting von Widersheim's close relations with Commander Leary. It is believed by Germans that the American officer resented what he took to be neglect. I mention this, not because I believe it to depict Commander Leary, but because it is typical of a prevailing infirmity among Germans in Samoa. Touchy themselves, they read all history in the light of personal affronts and tiffs; and I find this weakness indicated by the big thumb of Bismarck, when he places "sensitiveness to small disrespects—Empfindlichkeit ueber Mangel an Respect," among the causes of the wild career of Knappe. Whatever the cause, at least, the natives had no sooner taken arms than Leary appeared with violence upon that side. As early as the 3rd, he had sent an obscure but menacing despatch to Brandeis. On the 6th, he fell on Fritze in the matter of the Manono bombardment. "The revolutionists," he wrote, "had an armed force in the field within a few miles of this harbour, when the vessels under your command transported the Tamasese troops to a neighbouring island with the avowed intention of making war on the isolated homes of the women and children of the enemy. Being the only other representative of a naval power now present in this harbour, for the sake of humanity I hereby respectfully and solemnly protest in the name of the United States of America and of the civilised world in general against the use of a national war-vessel for such services as were yesterday rendered by the German corvette Adler." Fritze's reply, to the effect that he is under the orders of the consul and has no right of choice, reads even humble; perhaps he was not himself vain of the exploit, perhaps not prepared to see it thus described in words. From that moment Leary was in the front of the row. His name is diagnostic, but it was not required; on every step of his subsequent action in Samoa Irishman is writ large; over all his doings a malign spirit of humour presided. No malice was too small for him, if it were only funny. When night signals were made from Mulinuu, he would sit on his own poop and confound them with gratuitous rockets. He was at the pains to write a letter and address it to "the High Chief Tamasese"—a device as old at least as the wars of Robert Bruce—in order to bother the officials of the German post-office, in whose hands he persisted in leaving it, although the address was death to them and the distribution of letters in Samoa formed no part of their profession. His great masterwork of pleasantry, the Scanlon affair, must be narrated in its place. And he was no less bold than comical. The Adams was not supposed to be a match for the Adler; there was no glory to be gained in beating her; and yet I have heard naval officers maintain she might have proved a dangerous antagonist in narrow waters and at short range. Doubtless Leary thought so. He was continually daring Fritze to come on; and already, in a despatch of the 9th, I find Becker complaining of his language in the hearing of German officials, and how he had declared that, on the Adler again interfering, he would interfere himself, "if he went to the bottom for it—und wenn sein Schiff dabei zu Grunde ginge." Here is the style of opposition which has the merit of being frank, not that of being agreeable. Becker was annoying, Leary infuriating; there is no doubt that the tempers in the German consulate were highly ulcerated; and if war between the two countries did not follow, we must set down the praise to the forbearance of the German navy. This is not the last time that I shall have to salute the merits of that service.

The defeat and death of Saifaleupolu and the burning of Manono had thus passed off without the least advantage to Tamasese. But he still held the significant position of Mulinuu, and Brandeis was strenuous to make it good. The whole peninsula was surrounded with a breastwork; across the isthmus it was six feet high and strengthened with a ditch; and the beach was staked against landing. Weber's land claim—the same that now broods over the village in the form of a signboard—then appeared in a more military guise; the German flag was hoisted, and German sailors manned the breastwork at the isthmus—"to protect German property" and its trifling parenthesis, the king of Samoa. Much vigilance reigned and, in the island fashion, much wild firing. And in spite of all, desertion was for a long time daily. The detained high chiefs would go to the beach on the pretext of a natural occasion, plunge in the sea, and swimming across a broad, shallow bay of the lagoon, join the rebels on the Faleula side. Whole bodies of warriors, sometimes hundreds strong, departed with their arms and ammunition. On the 7th of September, for instance, the day after Leary's letter, Too and Mataia left with their contingents, and the whole Aana people returned home in a body to hold a parliament. Ten days later, it is true, a part of them returned to their duty; but another part branched off by the way and carried their services, and Tamasese's dear-bought guns, to Faleula.

On the 8th, there was a defection of a different kind, but yet sensible. The High Chief Seumanu had been still detained in Mulinuu under anxious observation. His people murmured at his absence, threatened to "take away his name," and had already attempted a rescue. The adventure was now taken in hand by his wife Faatulia, a woman of much sense and spirit and a strong partisan; and by her contrivance, Seumanu gave his guardians the slip and rejoined his clan at Faleula. This process of winnowing was of course counterbalanced by another of recruitment. But the harshness of European and military rule had made Brandeis detested and Tamasese unpopular with many; and the force on Mulinuu is thought to have done little more than hold its own. Mataafa sympathisers set it down at about two or three thousand. I have no estimate from the other side; but Becker admits they were not strong enough to keep the field in the open.

The political significance of Mulinuu was great, but in a military sense the position had defects. If it was difficult to carry, it was easy to blockade: and to be hemmed in on that narrow finger of land were an inglorious posture for the monarch of Samoa. The peninsula, besides, was scant of food and destitute of water. Pressed by these considerations, Brandeis extended his lines till he had occupied the whole foreshore of Apia bay and the opposite point, Matautu. His men were thus drawn out along some three nautical miles of irregular beach, everywhere with their backs to the sea, and without means of communication or mutual support except by water. The extension led to fresh sorrows. The Tamasese men quartered themselves in the houses of the absent men of the Vaimaunga. Disputes arose with English and Americans. Leary interposed in a loud voice of menace. It was said the firm profited by the confusion to buttress up imperfect land claims; I am sure the other whites would not be far behind the firm. Properties were fenced in, fences and houses were torn down, scuffles ensued. The German example at Mulinuu was followed with laughable unanimity; wherever an Englishman or an American conceived himself to have a claim, he set up the emblem of his country; and the beach twinkled with the flags of nations.

All this, it will be observed, was going forward in that neutral territory, sanctified by treaty against the presence of armed Samoans. The insurgents themselves looked on in wonder: on the 4th, trembling to transgress against the great Powers, they had written for a delimitation of the Eleele Sa; and Becker, in conversation with the British consul, replied that he recognised none. So long as Tamasese held the ground, this was expedient. But suppose Tamasese worsted, it might prove awkward for the stores, mills, and offices of a great German firm, thus bared of shelter by the act of their own consul.

On the morning of the 9th September, just ten days after the death of Saifaleupolu, Mataafa, under the name of Malietoa To'oa Mataafa, was crowned king at Faleula. On the 11th he wrote to the British and American consuls: "Gentlemen, I write this letter to you two very humbly and entreatingly, on account of this difficulty that has come before me. I desire to know from you two gentlemen the truth where the boundaries of the neutral territory are. You will observe that I am now at Vaimoso [a step nearer the enemy], and I have stopped here until I knew what you say regarding the neutral territory. I wish to know where I can go, and where the forbidden ground is, for I do not wish to go on any neutral territory, or on any foreigner's property. I do not want to offend any of the great Powers. Another thing I would like. Would it be possible for you three consuls to make Tamasese remove from German property? for I am in awe of going on German land." He must have received a reply embodying Becker's renunciation of the principle, at once; for he broke camp the same day, and marched eastward through the bush behind Apia.

Brandeis, expecting attack, sought to improve his indefensible position. He reformed his centre by the simple expedient of suppressing it. Apia was evacuated. The two flanks, Mulinuu and Matautu, were still held and fortified, Mulinuu (as I have said) to the isthmus, Matautu on a line from the bayside to the little river Fuisá. The centre was represented by the trajectory of a boat across the bay from one flank to another, and was held (we may say) by the German war-ship. Mataafa decided (I am assured) to make a feint on Matautu, induce Brandeis to deplete Mulinuu in support, and then fall upon and carry that. And there is no doubt in my mind that such a plan was bruited abroad, for nothing but a belief in it could explain the behaviour of Brandeis on the 12th. That it was seriously entertained by Mataafa I stoutly disbelieve; the German flag and sailors forbidding the enterprise in Mulinuu. So that we may call this false intelligence the beginning and the end of Mataafa's strategy.

The whites who sympathised with the revolt were uneasy and impatient. They will still tell you, though the dates are there to show them wrong, that Mataafa, even after his coronation, delayed extremely: a proof of how long two days may seem to last when men anticipate events. On the evening of the 11th, while the new king was already on the march, one of these walked into Matautu. The moon was bright. By the way he observed the native houses dark and silent; the men had been about a fortnight in the bush, but now the women and children were gone also; at which he wondered. On the sea-beach, in the camp of the Tamaseses, the solitude was near as great; he saw three or four men smoking before the British consulate, perhaps a dozen in all; the rest were behind in the bush upon their line of forts. About the midst he sat down, and here a woman drew near to him. The moon shone in her face, and he knew her for a householder near by, and a partisan of Mataafa's. She looked about her as she came, and asked him, trembling, what he did in the camp of Tamasese. He was there after news, he told her. She took him by the hand. "You must not stay here, you will get killed," she said. "The bush is full of our people, the others are watching them, fighting may begin at any moment, and we are both here too long." So they set off together; and she told him by the way that she had came to the hostile camp with a present of bananas, so that the Tamasese men might spare her house. By the Vaisingano they met an old man, a woman, and a child; and these also she warned and turned back. Such is the strange part played by women among the scenes of Samoan warfare, such were the liberties then permitted to the whites, that these two could pass the lines, talk together in

Tamasese's camp on the eve of an engagement, and pass forth again bearing intelligence, like privileged spies. And before a few hours the white man was in direct communication with the opposing general. The next morning he was accosted "about breakfast-time" by two natives who stood leaning against the pickets of a public-house, where the Siumu road strikes in at right angles to the main street of Apia. They told him battle was imminent, and begged him to pass a little way inland and speak with Mataafa. The road is at this point broad and fairly good, running between thick groves of cocoa-palm and breadfruit. A few hundred yards along this the white man passed a picket of four armed warriors, with red handkerchiefs and their faces blackened in the form of a full beard, the Mataafa rallying signs for the day; a little farther on, some fifty; farther still, a hundred; and at last a quarter of a mile of them sitting by the wayside armed and blacked.

Near by, in the verandah of a house on a knoll, he found Mataafa seated in white clothes, a Winchester across his knees. His men, he said, were still arriving from behind, and there was a turning movement in operation beyond the Fuisá, so that the Tamaseses should be assailed at the same moment from the south and east. And this is another indication that the attack on Matautu was the true attack; had any design on Mulinuu been in the wind, not even a Samoan general would have detached these troops upon the other side. While they still spoke, five Tamasese women were brought in with their hands bound; they had been stealing "our" bananas.

All morning the town was strangely deserted, the very children gone. A sense of expectation reigned, and sympathy for the attack was expressed publicly. Some men with unblacked faces came to Moors's store for biscuit. A native woman, who was there marketing, inquired after the news, and, hearing that the battle was now near at hand, "Give them two more tins," said she; "and don't put them down to my husband—he would growl; put them down to me." Between twelve and one, two white men walked toward Matautu, finding as they went no sign of war until they had passed the Vaisingano and come to the corner of a by-path leading to the bush. Here were four blackened warriors on guard,—the extreme left wing of the Mataafa force, where it touched the waters of the bay. Thence the line (which the white men followed) stretched inland among bush and marsh, facing the forts of the Tamaseses. The warriors lay as yet inactive behind trees; but all the young boys and harlots of Apia toiled in the front upon a trench, digging with knives and cocoa-shells; and a continuous stream of children brought them water. The young sappers worked crouching; from the outside only an occasional head, or a hand emptying a shell of earth, was visible; and their enemies looked on inert from the line of the opposing forts. The lists were not yet prepared, the tournament was not yet open; and the attacking force was suffered to throw up works under the silent guns of the defence. But there is an end even to the delay of islanders. As the white men stood and looked, the Tamasese line thundered into a volley; it was answered; the crowd of silent workers broke forth in laughter and cheers; and the battle had begun.

Thenceforward, all day and most of the next night, volley followed volley; and pounds of lead and pounds sterling of money continued to be blown into the air without cessation and almost without result. Colonel de Coetlogon, an old soldier, described the noise as deafening. The harbour was all struck with shots; a man was knocked over on the German war-ship; half Apia was under fire; and a house was pierced beyond the Mulivai. All along the two lines of breastwork, the entrenched enemies exchanged this hail of balls; and away on the east of the battle the fusillade was maintained, with equal spirit, across the narrow barrier of the Fuisá. The whole rear of the Tamaseses was enfiladed by this flank fire; and I have seen a house there, by the river brink, that was riddled with bullets like a piece of worm-eaten wreck-wood. At this point of the field befell a trait of Samoan warfare worth recording. Taiese (brother to Siteoni already mentioned) shot a Tamasese man. He saw him fall, and, inflamed with the lust of glory, passed the river single-handed in that storm of missiles to secure the head. On the farther bank, as was but natural, he fell himself; he who had gone to take a trophy remained to afford one; and the Mataafas, who had looked on exulting in the prospect of a triumph, saw themselves exposed instead to a disgrace. Then rose one Vingi, passed the deadly water, swung the body of Taiese on his back, and returned unscathed to his own side, the head saved, the corpse filled with useless bullets.

At this rate of practice, the ammunition soon began to run low, and from an early hour of the afternoon, the Malietoa stores were visited by customers in search of more. An elderly man came leaping and cheering, his gun in one hand, a basket of three heads in the other. A fellow came shot through the forearm. "It doesn't hurt now," he said, as he bought his cartridges; "but it will hurt to-morrow, and I want to fight while I can." A third followed, a mere boy, with the end of his nose shot off: "Have you any painkiller? give it me quick, so that I can get back to fight." On either side, there was the same delight in sound and smoke and schoolboy cheering, the same unsophisticated ardour of battle; and the misdirected skirmish proceeded with a din, and was illustrated with traits of bravery that would have fitted a Waterloo or a Sedan.

I have said how little I regard the alleged plan of battle. At least it was now all gone to water. The whole forces of Mataafa had leaked out, man by man, village by village, on the so-called false attack. They were all pounding for their lives on the front and the left flank of Matautu. About half-past three they enveloped the right flank also. The defenders were driven back along the beach road as far as the pilot station at the turn of the land. From this also they were dislodged, stubbornly fighting. One, it is told, retreated to his middle in the lagoon; stood there, loading and firing, till he fell; and his body was found on the morrow pierced with four mortal wounds. The Tamasese force was now enveloped on three sides; it was besides almost cut off from the sea; and across its whole rear and only way of retreat a fire of hostile bullets crossed from east and west, in the midst of which men were surprised to observe the birds continuing to sing, and a cow grazed all afternoon unhurt. Doubtless here was the defence in a poor way; but then the attack was in irons. For the Mataafas about the pilot house could scarcely advance beyond without coming under the fire of their own men from the other side of the Fuisá; and there was not enough organisation, perhaps not enough authority, to divert or to arrest that fire.

The progress of the fight along the beach road was visible from Mulinuu, and Brandeis despatched ten boats of reinforcements. They crossed the harbour, paused for a while beside the Adler—it is supposed for ammunition—and drew near the Matautu shore. The Mataafa men lay close among the shore-side bushes, expecting their arrival; when a silly lad, in mere lightness of heart, fired a shot in the air. My native friend, Mrs. Mary Hamilton, ran out of her house and gave the culprit a good shaking: an episode in the midst of battle as incongruous as the grazing cow. But his sillier comrades followed his example; a harmless volley warned the boats what they might expect; and they drew back and passed outside the reef for the passage of the Fuisá. Here they came under the fire of the right wing of the Mataafas on the river-bank. The beach, raked east and west, appeared to them no place to land on. And they hung off in the deep water of the lagoon inside the barrier reef, feebly fusillading the pilot house.

Between four and five, the Fabeata regiment (or folk of that village) on the Mataafa left, which had been under arms all day, fell to be withdrawn for rest and food; the Siumu regiment, which should have relieved it, was not ready or not notified in time; and the Tamaseses, gallantly profiting by the mismanagement, recovered the most of the ground in their proper right. It was not for long. They lost it again, yard by yard and from house to house, till the pilot station was once more in the hands of the Mataafas. This is the last definite incident in the battle. The vicissitudes along the line of the entrenchments remain concealed from us under the cover of the forest. Some part of the Tamasese position there appears to have been carried, but what part, or at what hour, or whether the advantage was maintained, I have never learned. Night and rain, but not silence, closed upon the field. The trenches were deep in mud; but the younger folk wrecked the houses in the neighbourhood, carried the roofs to the front, and lay under them, men and women together, through a long night of furious squalls and furious and useless volleys. Meanwhile the older folk trailed back into Apia in the rain; they talked as they went of who had fallen and what heads had been taken upon either side—they seemed to know by name the losses upon both; and drenched with wet and broken with excitement and fatigue, they crawled into the verandahs of the town to eat and sleep. The morrow broke grey and drizzly, but as so often happens in the islands, cleared up into a glorious day. During the night, the majority of the defenders had taken advantage of the rain and darkness and stolen from their forts unobserved. The rallying sign of the Tamaseses had been a white handkerchief. With the dawn, the de Coetlogons from the English consulate beheld the ground strewn with these badges discarded; and close by the house, a belated turncoat was still changing white for red. Matautu was lost; Tamasese was confined to Mulinuu; and by nine o'clock two Mataafa villages paraded the streets of Apia, taking possession. The cost of this respectable success in ammunition must have been enormous; in life it was but small. Some compute forty killed on either side, others forty on both, three or four being women and one a white man, master of a schooner from Fiji. Nor was the number even of the wounded at all proportionate to the surprising din and fury of the affair while it lasted.

CHAPTER VI—LAST EXPLOITS OF BECKER

September-November 1888

Brandeis had held all day by Mulinuu, expecting the reported real attack. He woke on the 13th to find himself cut off on that unwatered promontory, and the Mataafa villagers parading Apia. The same day Fritze received a letter from Mataafa summoning him to withdraw his party from the isthmus; and Fritze, as if in answer, drew in his ship into the small harbour close to Mulinuu, and trained his port battery to assist in the defence. From a step so decisive, it might be thought the German plans were unaffected by the disastrous issue of the battle. I conceive nothing would be further from the truth. Here was Tamasese penned on Mulinuu with his troops; Apia, from which alone these could be subsisted, in the hands of the enemy; a battle imminent, in which the German vessel must apparently take part with men and battery, and the buildings of the German firm were apparently destined to be the first target of fire. Unless Becker re-established that which he had so lately and so artfully thrown down—the neutral territory—the firm would have to suffer. If he re-established it, Tamasese must retire from Mulinuu. If Becker saved his goose, he lost his cabbage. Nothing so well depicts the man's effrontery as that he should have conceived the design of saving both,—of re-establishing only so much of the neutral territory as should hamper Mataafa, and leaving in abeyance all that could incommode Tamasese. By drawing the boundary where he now proposed, across the isthmus, he protected the firm, drove back the Mataafas out of almost all that they had conquered, and, so far from disturbing Tamasese, actually fortified him in his old position.

The real story of the negotiations that followed we shall perhaps never learn. But so much is plain: that while Becker was thus outwardly straining decency in the interest of Tamasese, he was privately intriguing, or pretending to intrigue, with Mataafa. In his despatch of the 11th, he had given an extended criticism of that chieftain, whom he depicts as very dark and artful; and while admitting that his assumption of the name of Malietoa might raise him up followers, predicted that he could not make an orderly government or support himself long in sole power "without very energetic foreign help." Of what help was the consul thinking? There was no helper in the field but Germany. On the 15th he had an interview with the victor; told him that Tamasese's was the only government recognised by Germany, and that he must continue to recognise it till he received "other instructions from his government, whom he was now advising of the late events"; refused, accordingly, to withdraw the guard from the isthmus; and desired Mataafa, "until the arrival of these fresh instructions," to refrain from an attack on Mulinuu. One thing of two: either this language is extremely perfidious, or Becker was preparing to change sides. The same detachment appears in his despatch of October 7th. He computes the losses of the German firm with an easy cheerfulness. If Tamasese get up again (gelingt die Wiederherstellung der Regierung Tamasese's), Tamasese will have to pay. If not, then Mataafa. This is not the language of a partisan. The tone of indifference, the easy implication that the case of Tamasese was already desperate, the hopes held secretly forth to Mataafa and secretly reported to his government at home, trenchantly contrast with his external conduct. At this very time he was feeding Tamasese; he had German sailors mounting guard on Tamasese's battlements; the German war-ship lay close in, whether to help or to destroy. If he meant to drop the cause of Tamasese, he had him in a corner, helpless, and could stifle him without a sob. If he meant to rat, it was to be with every condition of safety and every circumstance of infamy.

Was it conceivable, then, that he meant it? Speaking with a gentleman who was in the confidence of Dr. Knappe: "Was it not a pity," I asked, "that Knappe did not stick to Becker's policy of supporting Mataafa?" "You are quite wrong there; that was not Knappe's doing," was the reply. "Becker had changed his mind before Knappe came." Why, then, had he changed it? This excellent, if ignominious, idea once entertained, why was it let drop? It is to be remembered there was another German in the field, Brandeis, who had a respect, or rather, perhaps, an affection, for Tamasese, and who thought his own honour and that of his country engaged in the support of that government which they had provoked and founded. Becker described the captain to Laupepa as "a quiet, sensible gentleman." If any word came to his ears of the intended manoeuvre, Brandeis would certainly show himself very sensible of the affront; but Becker might have been tempted to withdraw his former epithet of quiet. Some such passage, some such threatened change of front at the consulate, opposed with outcry, would explain what seems otherwise inexplicable, the bitter, indignant, almost hostile tone of a subsequent letter from Brandeis to Knappe—"Brandeis's inflammatory letter," Bismarck calls it—the proximate cause of the German landing and reverse at Fangalii.

But whether the advances of Becker were sincere or not—whether he meditated treachery against the old king or was practising treachery upon the new, and the choice is between one or other—no doubt but he contrived to gain his points with Mataafa, prevailing on him to change his camp for the better protection of the German plantations, and persuading him (long before he could persuade his brother consuls) to accept that miraculous new neutral territory of his, with a piece cut out for the immediate needs of Tamasese.

During the rest of September, Tamasese continued to decline. On the 19th one village and half of another deserted him; on the 22nd two more. On the 21st the Mataafas burned his town of Leulumoenga, his own splendid house flaming with the rest; and there are few things of which a native thinks more, or has more reason to think well, than of a fine Samoan house. Tamasese women and children were marched up the same day from Atua, and handed over with their sleeping-mats to Mulinuu: a most unwelcome addition to a party already suffering from want. By the 20th, they were being watered from the Adler. On the 24th the Manono fleet of sixteen large boats, fortified and rendered unmanageable with tons of firewood, passed to windward to intercept supplies from Atua. By the 27th the hungry garrison flocked in great numbers to draw rations at the German firm. On the 28th the same business was repeated with a different issue. Mataafas crowded to look on; words were exchanged, blows followed; sticks, stones, and bottles were caught up; the detested Brandeis, at great risk, threw himself between the lines and expostulated with the Mataafas—his only personal appearance in the wars, if this could be called war. The same afternoon, the Tamasese boats got in with provisions, having passed to seaward of the lumbering Manono fleet; and from that day on, whether from a high degree of enterprise on the one side or a great lack of capacity on the other, supplies were maintained from the sea with regularity. Thus the spectacle of battle, or at least of riot, at the doors of the German firm was not repeated. But the memory must have hung heavy on the hearts, not of the Germans only, but of all Apia. The Samoans are a gentle race, gentler than any in Europe; we are often enough reminded of the circumstance, not always by their friends. But a mob is a mob, and a drunken mob is a drunken mob, and a drunken mob with weapons in its hands is a drunken mob with weapons in its hands, all the world over: elementary propositions, which some of us upon these islands might do worse than get by rote, but which must have been evident enough to Becker. And I am amazed by the man's constancy, that, even while blows were going at the door of that German firm which he was in Samoa to protect, he should have stuck to his demands. Ten days before, Blacklock had offered to recognise the old territory, including Mulinuu, and Becker had refused, and still in the midst of these "alarums and excursions," he continued to refuse it.

On October 2nd, anchored in Apia bay H.B.M.S. Calliope, Captain Kane, carrying the flag of Rear-Admiral Fairfax, and the gunboat Lizard, Lieutenant-Commander Pelly. It was rumoured the admiral had come to recognise the government of Tamasese, I believe in error. And at least the day for that was quite gone by; and he arrived not to salute the king's accession, but to arbitrate on his remains. A conference of the consuls and commanders met on board the Calliope, October 4th, Fritze alone being absent, although twice invited: the affair touched politics, his consul was to be there; and even if he came to the meeting (so he explained to Fairfax) he would have no voice in its deliberations. The parties were plainly marked out: Blacklock and Leary maintaining their offer of the old neutral territory, and probably willing to expand or to contract it to any conceivable extent, so long as Mulinuu was still included; Knappe offered (if the others liked) to include "the whole eastern end of the island," but quite fixed upon the one point that Mulinuu should be left out; the English willing to meet either view, and singly desirous that Apia should be neutralised. The conclusion was foregone. Becker held a trump card in the consent of Mataafa; Blacklock and Leary stood alone, spoke with all ill grace, and could not long hold out. Becker had his way; and the neutral boundary was chosen just where he desired: across the isthmus, the firm within, Mulinuu without. He did not long enjoy the fruits of victory.

On the 7th, three days after the meeting, one of the Scanlons (well-known and intelligent half-castes) came to Blacklock with a complaint. The Scanlon house stood on the hither side of the Tamasese breastwork, just inside the newly accepted territory, and within easy range of the firm. Armed men, to the number of a hundred, had issued from Mulinuu, had "taken charge" of the house, had pointed a gun at Scanlon's head, and had twice "threatened to kill" his pigs. I hear elsewhere of some effects (Gegenstände) removed. At the best a very pale atrocity, though we shall find the word employed. Germans declare besides that Scanlon was no American subject; they declare the point had been decided by court-martial in 1875; that Blacklock had the decision in the consular archives; and that this was his reason for handing the affair to Leary. It is not necessary to suppose so. It is plain he thought little of the business; thought indeed nothing of it; except in so far as armed men had entered the neutral territory from Mulinuu; and it was on this ground alone, and the implied breach of Becker's engagement at the conference, that he invited Leary's attention to the tale. The impish ingenuity of the commander perceived in it huge possibilities of mischief. He took up the Scanlon outrage, the atrocity of the threatened pigs; and with that poor instrument—I am sure, to his own wonder—drove Tamasese out of Mulinuu. It was "an intrigue," Becker complains. To be sure it was; but who was Becker to be complaining of intrigue?

On the 7th Leary laid before Fritze the following conundrum: "As the natives of Mulinuu appear to be under the protection of the Imperial German naval guard belonging to the vessel under your command, I have the honour to request you to inform me whether or not they are under such protection? Amicable relations," pursued the humorist, "amicable relations exist between the government of the United States and His Imperial German Majesty's government, but we do not recognise Tamasese's government, and I am desirous of locating the responsibility for violations of American rights." Becker and Fritze lost no time in explanation or denial, but went straight to the root of the matter and sought to buy off Scanlon. Becker declares that every reparation was offered. Scanlon takes a pride to recapitulate the leases and the situations he refused, and the long interviews in which he was tempted and plied with drink by Becker or Beckmann of the firm. No doubt, in short, that he was offered reparation in reason and out of reason, and, being thoroughly primed, refused it all. Meantime some answer must be made to Leary; and Fritze repeated on the 8th his oft-repeated assurances that he was not authorised to deal with politics. The same day Leary retorted: "The question is not one of diplomacy nor of politics. It is strictly one of military jurisdiction and responsibility. Under the shadow of the German fort at Mulinuu," continued the hyperbolical commander, "atrocities have been committed. . . . And I again have the honour respectfully to request to be informed whether or not the armed natives at Mulinuu are under the protection of the Imperial German naval guard belonging to the vessel under your command." To this no answer was vouchsafed till the 11th, and then in the old terms; and meanwhile, on the 10th, Leary got into his gaiters—the sure sign, as was both said and sung aboard his vessel, of some desperate or some amusing service—and was set ashore at the Scanlons' house. Of this he took possession at the head of an old woman and a mop, and was seen from the Tamasese breastwork directing operations and plainly preparing to install himself there in a military posture. So much he meant to be understood; so much he meant to carry out, and an armed party from the Adams was to have garrisoned on the morrow the scene of the atrocity. But there is no doubt he managed to convey more. No doubt he was a master in the art of loose speaking, and could always manage to be overheard when he wanted; and by this, or some other equally unofficial means, he spread the rumour that on the morrow he was to bombard.

The proposed post, from its position, and from Leary's well-established character as an artist in mischief, must have been regarded by the Germans with uneasiness. In the bombardment we can scarce suppose them to have believed. But Tamasese must have both believed and trembled. The prestige of the European Powers was still unbroken. No native would then have dreamed of defying these colossal ships, worked by mysterious powers, and laden with outlandish instruments of death. None would have dreamed of resisting those strange but quite unrealised Great Powers, understood (with difficulty) to be larger than Tonga and Samoa put together, and known to be prolific of prints, knives, hard biscuit, picture-books, and other luxuries, as well as of overbearing men and inconsistent orders. Laupepa had fallen in ill-blood with one of them; his only idea of defence had been to throw himself in the arms of another; his name, his rank, and his great following had not been able to preserve him; and he had vanished from the eyes of men—as the Samoan thinks of it, beyond the sky. Asi, Maunga, Tuiletu-funga, had followed him in that new path of doom. We have seen how carefully Mataafa still walked, how he dared not set foot on the neutral territory till assured it was no longer sacred, how he withdrew from it again as soon as its sacredness had been restored, and at the bare word of a consul (however gilded with ambiguous promises) paused in his course of victory and left his rival unassailed in Mulinuu. And now it was the rival's turn. Hitherto happy in the continued support of one of the white Powers, he now found himself—or thought himself—threatened with war by no less than two others.

Tamasese boats as they passed Matautu were in the habit of firing on the shore, as like as not without particular aim, and more in high spirits than hostility. One of these shots pierced the house of a British subject near the consulate; the consul reported to Admiral Fairfax; and, on the morning of the 10th, the admiral despatched Captain Kane of the Calliope to Mulinuu. Brandeis met the messenger with voluble excuses and engagements for the future. He was told his explanations were satisfactory so far as they went, but that the admiral's message was to Tamasese, the de facto king. Brandeis, not very well assured of his puppet's courage, attempted in vain to excuse him from appearing. No de facto king, no message, he was told: produce your de facto king. And Tamasese had at last to be produced. To him Kane delivered his errand: that the Lizard was to remain for the protection of British subjects; that a signalman was to be stationed at the consulate; that, on any further firing from boats, the signalman was to notify the Lizard and she to fire one gun, on which all boats must lower sail and come alongside for examination and the detection of the guilty; and that, "in the event of the boats not obeying the gun, the admiral would not be responsible for the consequences." It was listened to by Brandeis and Tamasese "with the greatest attention." Brandeis, when it was done, desired his thanks to the admiral for the moderate terms of his message, and, as Kane went to his boat, repeated the expression of his gratitude as though he meant it, declaring his own hands would be thus strengthened for the maintenance of discipline. But I have yet to learn of any gratitude on the part of Tamasese. Consider the case of the poor owlish man hearing for the first time our diplomatic commonplaces. The admiral would not be answerable for the consequences. Think of it! A devil of a position for a de facto king. And here, the same afternoon, was Leary in the Scanlon house, mopping it out for unknown designs by the hands of an old woman, and proffering strange threats of bloodshed. Scanlon and his pigs, the admiral and his gun, Leary and his bombardment,—what a kettle of fish!

I dwell on the effect on Tamasese. Whatever the faults of Becker, he was not timid; he had already braved so much for Mulinuu that I cannot but think he might have continued to hold up his head even after the outrage of the pigs, and that the weakness now shown originated with the king. Late in the night, Blacklock was wakened to receive a despatch addressed to Leary. "You have asked that I and my government go away from Mulinuu, because you pretend a man who lives near Mulinuu and who is under your protection, has been threatened by my soldiers. As your Excellency has forbidden the man to accept any satisfaction, and as I do not wish to make war against the United States, I shall remove my government from Mulinuu to another place." It was signed by Tamasese, but I think more heads than his had wagged over the direct and able letter. On the morning of the 11th, accordingly, Mulinuu the much defended lay desert. Tamasese and Brandeis had slipped to sea in a schooner; their troops had followed them in boats; the German sailors and their war-flag had returned on board the Adler; and only the German merchant flag blew there for Weber's land-claim. Mulinuu, for which Becker had intrigued so long and so often, for which he had overthrown the municipality, for which he had abrogated and refused and invented successive schemes of neutral territory, was now no more to the Germans than a very unattractive, barren peninsula and a very much disputed land-claim of Mr. Weber's. It will scarcely be believed that the tale of the Scanlon outrages was not yet finished. Leary had gained his point, but Scanlon had lost his compensation. And it was months later, and this time in the shape of a threat of bombardment in black and white, that Tamasese heard the last of the absurd affair. Scanlon had both his fun and his money, and Leary's practical joke was brought to an artistic end.

Becker sought and missed an instant revenge. Mataafa, a devout Catholic, was in the habit of walking every morning to mass from his camp at Vaiala beyond Matautu to the mission at the Mulivai. He was sometimes escorted by as many as six guards in uniform, who displayed their proficiency in drill by perpetually shifting arms as they marched. Himself, meanwhile, paced in front, bareheaded and barefoot, a staff in his hand, in the customary chief's dress of white kilt, shirt, and jacket, and with a conspicuous rosary about his neck. Tall but not heavy, with eager eyes and a marked appearance of courage and capacity, Mataafa makes an admirable figure in the eyes of Europeans; to those of his countrymen, he may seem not always to preserve that quiescence of manner which is thought becoming in the great. On the morning of October 16th he reached the mission before day with two attendants, heard mass, had coffee with the fathers, and left again in safety. The smallness of his following we may suppose to have been reported. He was scarce gone, at least, before Becker had armed men at the mission gate and came in person seeking him.

The failure of this attempt doubtless still further exasperated the consul, and he began to deal as in an enemy's country. He had marines from the Adler to stand sentry over the consulate and parade the streets by threes and fours. The bridge of the Vaisingano, which cuts in half the English and American quarters, he closed by proclamation and advertised for tenders to demolish it. On the 17th Leary and Pelly landed carpenters and repaired it in his teeth. Leary, besides, had marines under arms, ready to land them if it should be necessary to protect the work. But Becker looked on without interference, perhaps glad enough to have the bridge repaired; for even Becker may not always have offended intentionally. Such was now the distracted posture of the little town: all government extinct, the German consul patrolling it with armed men and issuing proclamations like a ruler, the two other Powers defying his commands, and at least one of them prepared to use force in the defiance. Close on its skirts sat the warriors of Mataafa, perhaps four thousand strong, highly incensed against the Germans, having all to gain in the seizure of the town and firm, and, like an army in a fairy tale, restrained by the air-drawn boundary of the neutral ground.

I have had occasion to refer to the strange appearance in these islands of an American adventurer with a battery of cannon. The adventurer was long since gone, but his guns remained, and one of them was now to make fresh history. It had been cast overboard by Brandeis on the outer reef in the course of this retreat; and word of it coming to the ears of the Mataafas, they thought it natural that they should serve themselves the heirs of Tamasese. On the 23rd a Manono boat of the kind called taumualua dropped down the coast from Mataafa's camp, called in broad day at the German quarter of the town for guides, and proceeded to the reef. Here, diving with a rope, they got the gun aboard; and the night being then come, returned by the same route in the shallow water along shore, singing a boat-song. It will be seen with what childlike reliance they had accepted the neutrality of Apia bay; they came for the gun without concealment, laboriously dived for it in broad day under the eyes of the town and shipping, and returned with it, singing as they went. On Grevsmühl's wharf, a light showed them a crowd of German blue-jackets clustered, and a hail was heard. "Stop the singing so that we may hear what is said," said one of the chiefs in the taumualua. The song ceased; the hail was heard again, "Au mai le fana—bring the gun"; and the natives report themselves to have replied in the affirmative, and declare that they had begun to back the boat. It is perhaps not needful to believe them. A volley at least was fired from the wharf, at about fifty yards' range and with a very ill direction, one bullet whistling over Pelly's head on board the Lizard. The natives jumped overboard; and swimming under the lee of the taumualua (where they escaped a second volley) dragged her towards the east. As soon as they were out of range and past the Mulivai, the German border, they got on board and (again singing—though perhaps a different song) continued their return along the English and American shore. Off Matautu they were hailed from the seaward by one of the Adler's boats, which had been suddenly despatched on the sound of the firing or had stood ready all evening to secure the gun. The hail was in German; the Samoans knew not what it meant, but took the precaution to jump overboard and swim for land. Two volleys and some dropping shot were poured upon them in the water; but they dived, scattered, and came to land unhurt in different quarters of Matautu. The volleys, fired inshore, raked the highway, a British house was again pierced by numerous bullets, and these sudden sounds of war scattered consternation through the town.

Two British subjects, Hetherington-Carruthers, a solicitor, and Maben, a land-surveyor—the first being in particular a man well versed in the native mind and language—hastened at once to their consul; assured him the Mataafas would be roused to fury by this onslaught in the neutral zone, that the German quarter would be certainly attacked, and the rest of the town and white inhabitants exposed to a peril very difficult of estimation; and prevailed upon him to intrust them with a mission to the king. By the time they reached headquarters, the warriors were already taking post round Matafele, and the agitation of Mataafa himself was betrayed in the fact that he spoke with the deputation standing and gun in hand: a breach of high-chief dignity perhaps unparalleled. The usual result, however, followed: the whites persuaded the Samoan; and the attack was countermanded, to the benefit of all concerned, and not least of Mataafa. To the benefit of all, I say; for I do not think the Germans were that evening in a posture to resist; the liquor-cellars of the firm must have fallen into the power of the insurgents; and I will repeat my formula that a mob is a mob, a drunken mob is a drunken mob, and a drunken mob with weapons in its hands is a drunken mob with weapons in its hands, all the world over.

In the opinion of some, then, the town had narrowly escaped destruction, or at least the miseries of a drunken sack. To the knowledge of all, the air of the neutral territory had once more whistled with bullets. And it was clear the incident must have diplomatic consequences. Leary and Pelly both protested to Fritze. Leary announced he should report the affair to his government "as a gross violation of the principles of international law, and as a breach of the neutrality." "I positively decline the protest," replied Fritze, "and cannot fail to express my astonishment at the tone of your last letter." This was trenchant. It may be said, however, that Leary was already out of court; that, after the night signals and the Scanlon incident, and so many other acts of practical if humorous hostility, his position as a neutral was no better than a doubtful jest. The case with Pelly was entirely different; and with Pelly, Fritze was less well inspired. In his first note, he was on the old guard; announced that he had acted on the requisition of his consul, who was alone responsible on "the legal side"; and declined accordingly to discuss "whether the lives of British subjects were in danger, and to what extent armed intervention was necessary." Pelly replied judiciously that he had nothing to do with political matters, being only responsible for the safety of Her Majesty's ships under his command and for the lives and property of British subjects; that he had considered his protest a purely naval one; and as the matter stood could only report the case to the admiral on the station. "I have the honour," replied Fritze, "to refuse to entertain the protest concerning the safety of Her Britannic Majesty's ship Lizard as being a naval matter. The safety of Her Majesty's ship Lizard was never in the least endangered. This was guaranteed by the disciplined fire of a few shots under the direction of two officers." This offensive note, in view of Fritze's careful and honest bearing among so many other complications, may be attributed to some misunderstanding. His small knowledge of English perhaps failed him. But I cannot pass it by without remarking how far too much it is the custom of German officials to fall into this style. It may be witty, I am sure it is not wise. It may be sometimes necessary to offend for a definite object, it can never be diplomatic to offend gratuitously.

Becker was more explicit, although scarce less curt. And his defence may be divided into two statements: first, that the taumualua was proceeding to land with a hostile purpose on Mulinuu; second, that the shots complained of were fired by the Samoans. The second may be dismissed with a laugh. Human nature has laws. And no men hitherto discovered, on being suddenly challenged from the sea, would have turned their backs upon the challenger and poured volleys on the friendly shore. The first is not extremely credible, but merits examination. The story of the recovered gun seems straightforward; it is supported by much testimony, the diving operations on the reef seem to have been watched from shore with curiosity; it is hard to suppose that it does not roughly represent the fact. And yet if any part of it be true, the whole of Becker's explanation falls to the ground. A boat which had skirted the whole eastern coast of Mulinuu, and was already opposite a wharf in Matafele, and still going west, might have been guilty on a thousand points—there was one on which she was necessarily innocent; she was necessarily innocent of proceeding on Mulinuu. Or suppose the diving operations, and the native testimony, and Pelly's chart of the boat's course, and the boat itself, to be all stages of some epidemic hallucination or steps in a conspiracy—suppose even a second taumualua to have entered Apia bay after nightfall, and to have been fired upon from Grevsmühl's wharf in the full career of hostilities against Mulinuu—suppose all this, and Becker is not helped. At the time of the first fire, the boat was off Grevsmühl's wharf. At the time of the second (and that is the one complained of) she was off Carruthers's wharf in Matautu. Was she still proceeding on Mulinuu? I trow not. The danger to German property was no longer imminent, the shots had been fired upon a very trifling provocation, the spirit implied was that of designed disregard to the neutrality. Such was the impression here on the spot; such in plain terms the statement of Count Hatzfeldt to Lord Salisbury at home: that the neutrality of Apia was only "to prevent the natives from fighting," not the Germans; and that whatever Becker might have promised at the conference, he could not "restrict German war-vessels in their freedom of action."

There was nothing to surprise in this discovery; and had events been guided at the same time with a steady and discreet hand, it might have passed with less observation. But the policy of Becker was felt to be not only reckless, it was felt to be absurd also. Sudden nocturnal onfalls upon native boats could lead, it was felt, to no good end whether of peace or war; they could but exasperate; they might prove, in a moment, and when least expected, ruinous. To those who knew how nearly it had come to fighting, and who considered the probable result, the future looked ominous. And fear was mingled with annoyance in the minds of the Anglo-Saxon colony. On the 24th, a public meeting appealed to the British and American consuls. At half-past seven in the evening guards were landed at the consulates. On the morrow they were each fortified with sand-bags; and the subjects informed by proclamation that these asylums stood open to them on any alarm, and at any hour of the day or night. The social bond in Apia was dissolved. The consuls, like barons of old, dwelt each in his armed citadel. The rank and file of the white nationalities dared each other, and sometimes fell to on the street like rival clansmen. And the little town, not by any fault of the inhabitants, rather by the act of Becker, had fallen back in civilisation about a thousand years.

There falls one more incident to be narrated, and then I can close with this ungracious chapter. I have mentioned the name of the new English consul. It is already familiar to English readers; for the gentleman who was fated to undergo some strange experiences in Apia was the same de Coetlogon who covered Hicks's flank at the time of the disaster in the desert, and bade farewell to Gordon in Khartoum before the investment. The colonel was abrupt and testy; Mrs. de Coetlogon was too exclusive for society like that of Apia; but whatever their superficial disabilities, it is strange they should have left, in such an odour of unpopularity, a place where they set so shining an example of the sterling virtues. The colonel was perhaps no diplomatist; he was certainly no lawyer; but he discharged the duties of his office with the constancy and courage of an old soldier, and these were found sufficient. He and his wife had no ambition to be the leaders of society; the consulate was in their time no house of feasting; but they made of it that house of mourning to which the preacher tells us it is better we should go. At an early date after the battle of Matautu, it was opened as a hospital for the wounded. The English and Americans subscribed what was required for its support. Pelly of the Lizard strained every nerve to help, and set up tents on the lawn to be a shelter for the patients. The doctors of the English and American ships, and in particular Dr. Oakley of the Lizard, showed themselves indefatigable. But it was on the de Coetlogons that the distress fell. For nearly half a year, their lawn, their verandah, sometimes their rooms, were cumbered with the sick and dying, their ears were filled with the complaints of suffering humanity, their time was too short for the multiplicity of pitiful duties. In Mrs. de Coetlogon, and her helper, Miss Taylor, the merit of this endurance was perhaps to be looked for; in a man of the colonel's temper, himself painfully suffering, it was viewed with more surprise, if with no more admiration. Doubtless all had their reward in a sense of duty done; doubtless, also, as the days passed, in the spectacle of many traits of gratitude and patience, and in the success that waited on their efforts. Out of a hundred cases treated, only five died. They were all well-behaved, though full of childish wiles. One old gentleman, a high chief, was seized with alarming symptoms of belly-ache whenever Mrs. de Coetlogon went her rounds at night: he was after brandy.

Others were insatiable for morphine or opium. A chief woman had her foot amputated under chloroform. "Let me see my foot! Why does it not hurt?" she cried. "It hurt so badly before I went to sleep." Siteoni, whose name has been already mentioned, had his shoulder-blade excised, lay the longest of any, perhaps behaved the worst, and was on all these grounds the favourite. At times he was furiously irritable, and would rail upon his family and rise in bed until he swooned with pain. Once on the balcony he was thought to be dying, his family keeping round his mat, his father exhorting him to be prepared, when Mrs. de Coetlogon brought him round again with brandy and smelling-salts. After discharge, he returned upon a visit of gratitude; and it was observed, that instead of coming straight to the door, he went and stood long under his umbrella on that spot of ground where his mat had been stretched and he had endured pain so many months. Similar visits were the rule, I believe without exception; and the grateful patients loaded Mrs. de Coetlogon with gifts which (had that been possible in Polynesia) she would willingly have declined, for they were often of value to the givers.

The tissue of my story is one of rapacity, intrigue, and the triumphs of temper; the hospital at the consulate stands out almost alone as an episode of human beauty, and I dwell on it with satisfaction. But it was not regarded at the time with universal favour; and even to-day its institution is thought by many to have been impolitic. It was opened, it stood open, for the wounded of either party. As a matter of fact it was never used but by the Mataafas, and the Tamaseses were cared for exclusively by German doctors. In the progressive decivilisation of the town, these duties of humanity became thus a ground of quarrel. When the Mataafa hurt were first brought together after the battle of Matautu, and some more or less amateur surgeons were dressing wounds on a green by the wayside, one from the German consulate went by in the road. "Why don't you let the dogs die?" he asked. "Go to hell," was the rejoinder. Such were the amenities of Apia. But Becker reserved for himself the extreme expression of this spirit. On November 7th hostilities began again between the Samoan armies, and an inconclusive skirmish sent a fresh crop of wounded to the de Coetlogons. Next door to the consulate, some native houses and a chapel (now ruinous) stood on a green. Chapel and houses were certainly Samoan, but the ground was under a land-claim of the German firm; and de Coetlogon wrote to Becker requesting permission (in case it should prove necessary) to use these structures for his wounded. Before an answer came, the hospital was startled by the appearance of a case of gangrene, and the patient was hastily removed into the chapel. A rebel laid on German ground—here was an atrocity! The day before his own relief, November 11th, Becker ordered the man's instant removal. By his aggressive carriage and singular mixture of violence and cunning, he had already largely brought about the fall of Brandeis, and forced into an attitude of hostility the whole non-German population of the islands. Now, in his last hour of office, by this wanton buffet to his English colleague, he prepared a continuance of evil days for his successor. If the object of diplomacy be the organisation of failure in the midst of hate, he was a great diplomatist. And amongst a certain party on the beach he is still named as the ideal consul.

CHAPTER VII—THE SAMOAN CAMPS

November 1888

When Brandeis and Tamasese fled by night from Mulinuu, they carried their wandering government some six miles to windward, to a position above Lotoanuu. For some three miles to the eastward of Apia, the shores of Upolu are low and the ground rises with a gentle acclivity, much of which waves with German plantations. A barrier reef encloses a lagoon passable for boats: and the traveller skims there, on smooth, many-tinted shallows, between the wall of the breakers on the one hand, and on the other a succession of palm-tree capes and cheerful beach-side villages. Beyond the great plantation of Vailele, the character of the coast is changed. The barrier reef abruptly ceases, the surf beats direct upon the shore; and the mountains and untenanted forest of the interior descend sheer into the sea. The first mountain promontory is Letongo. The bay beyond is called Laulii, and became the headquarters of Mataafa. And on the next projection, on steep, intricate ground, veiled in forest and cut up by gorges and defiles, Tamasese fortified his lines. This greenwood citadel, which proved impregnable by Samoan arms, may be regarded as his front; the sea covered his right; and his rear extended along the coast as far as Saluafata, and thus commanded and drew upon a rich country, including the plain of Falefá.

He was left in peace from 11th October till November 6th. But his adversary is not wholly to be blamed for this delay, which depended upon island etiquette. His Savaii contingent had not yet come in, and to have moved again without waiting for them would have been surely to offend, perhaps to lose them. With the month of November they began to arrive: on the 2nd twenty boats, on the 3rd twenty-nine, on the 5th seventeen. On the 6th the position Mataafa had so long occupied on the skirts of Apia was deserted; all that day and night his force kept streaming eastward to Laulii; and on the 7th the siege of Lotoanuu was opened with a brisk skirmish.

Each side built forts, facing across the gorge of a brook. An endless fusillade and shouting maintained the spirit of the warriors; and at night, even if the firing slackened, the pickets continued to exchange from either side volleys of songs and pungent pleasantries. Nearer hostilities were rendered difficult by the nature of the ground, where men must thread dense bush and clamber on the face of precipices. Apia was near enough; a man, if he had a dollar or two, could walk in before a battle and array himself in silk or velvet. Casualties were not common; there was nothing to cast gloom upon the camps, and no more danger than was required to give a spice to the perpetual firing. For the young warriors it was a period of admirable enjoyment. But the anxiety of Mataafa must have been great and growing. His force was now considerable. It was scarce likely he should ever have more. That he should be long able to supply them with ammunition seemed incredible; at the rates then or soon after current, hundreds of pounds sterling might be easily blown into the air by the skirmishers in the course of a few days. And in the meanwhile, on the mountain opposite, his outnumbered adversary held his ground unshaken.

By this time the partisanship of the whites was unconcealed. Americans supplied Mataafa with ammunition; English and Americans openly subscribed together and sent boat-loads of provisions to his camp. One such boat started from Apia on a day of rain; it was pulled by six oars, three being paid by Moors, three by the MacArthurs; Moors himself and a clerk of the MacArthurs' were in charge; and the load included not only beef and biscuit, but three or four thousand rounds of ammunition. They came ashore in Laulii, and carried the gift to Mataafa. While they were yet in his house a bullet passed overhead; and out of his door they could see the Tamasese pickets on the opposite hill. Thence they made their way to the left flank of the Mataafa position next the sea. A Tamasese barricade was visible across the stream. It rained, but the warriors crowded in their shanties, squatted in the mud, and maintained an excited conversation. Balls flew; either faction, both happy as lords, spotting for the other in chance shots, and missing. One point is characteristic of that war; experts in native feeling doubt if it will characterise the next. The two white visitors passed without and between the lines to a rocky point upon the beach. The person of Moors was well known; the purpose of their coming to Laulii must have been already bruited abroad;

yet they were not fired upon. From the point they spied a crow's nest, or hanging fortification, higher up; and, judging it was a good position for a general view, obtained a guide. He led them up a steep side of the mountain, where they must climb by roots and tufts of grass; and coming to an open hill-top with some scattered trees, bade them wait, let him draw the fire, and then be swift to follow. Perhaps a dozen balls whistled about him ere he had crossed the dangerous passage and dropped on the farther side into the crow's-nest; the white men, briskly following, escaped unhurt. The crow's-nest was built like a bartizan on the precipitous front of the position. Across the ravine, perhaps at five hundred yards, heads were to be seen popping up and down in a fort of Tamesese's. On both sides the same enthusiasm without council, the same senseless vigilance, reigned. Some took aim; some blazed before them at a venture. Now—when a head showed on the other side—one would take a crack at it, remarking that it would never do to "miss a chance." Now they would all fire a volley and bob down; a return volley rang across the ravine, and was punctually answered: harmless as lawn-tennis. The whites expostulated in vain. The warriors, drunken with noise, made answer by a fresh general discharge and bade their visitors run while it was time. Upon their return to headquarters, men were covering the front with sheets of coral limestone, two balls having passed through the house in the interval. Mataafa sat within, over his kava bowl, unmoved. The picture is of a piece throughout: excellent courage, super-excellent folly, a war of school-children; expensive guns and cartridges used like squibs or catherine-wheels on Guy Fawkes's Day.

On the 20th Mataafa changed his attack. Tamasese's front was seemingly impregnable. Something must be tried upon his rear. There was his bread-basket; a small success in that direction would immediately curtail his resources; and it might be possible with energy to roll up his line along the beach and take the citadel in reverse. The scheme was carried out as might be expected from these childish soldiers. Mataafa, always uneasy about Apia, clung with a portion of his force to Laulii; and thus, had the foe been enterprising, exposed himself to disaster. The expedition fell successfully enough on Saluafata and drove out the Tamaseses with a loss of four heads; but so far from improving the advantage, yielded immediately to the weakness of the Samoan warrior, and ranged farther east through unarmed populations, bursting with shouts and blackened faces into villages terrified or admiring, making spoil of pigs, burning houses, and destroying gardens. The Tamasese had at first evacuated several beach towns in succession, and were still in retreat on Lotoanuu; finding themselves unpursued, they reoccupied them one after another, and re-established their lines to the very borders of Saluafata. Night fell; Mataafa had taken Saluafata, Tamasese had lost it; and that was all. But the day came near to have a different and very singular issue. The village was not long in the hands of the Mataafas, when a schooner, flying German colours, put into the bay and was immediately surrounded by their boats. It chanced that Brandeis was on board. Word of it had gone abroad, and the boats as they approached demanded him with threats. The late premier, alone, entirely unarmed, and a prey to natural and painful feelings, concealed himself below. The captain of the schooner remained on deck, pointed to the German colours, and defied approaching boats. Again the prestige of a great Power triumphed; the Samoans fell back before the bunting; the schooner worked out of the bay; Brandeis escaped. He himself apprehended the worst if he fell into Samoan hands; it is my diffident impression that his life would have been safe.

On the 22nd, a new German war-ship, the Eber, of tragic memory, came to Apia from the Gilberts, where she had been disarming turbulent islands. The rest of that day and all night she loaded stores from the firm, and on the morrow reached Saluafata bay. Thanks to the misconduct of the Mataafas, the most of the foreshore was still in the hands of the Tamaseses; and they were thus able to receive from the Eber both the stores and weapons. The weapons had been sold long since to Tarawa, Apaiang, and Pleasant Island; places unheard of by the general reader, where obscure inhabitants paid for these instruments of death in money or in labour, misused them as it was known they would be misused, and had been disarmed by force. The Eber had brought back the guns to a German counter, whence many must have been originally sold; and was here engaged, like a shopboy, in their distribution to fresh purchasers. Such is the vicious circle of the traffic in weapons of war. Another aid of a more metaphysical nature was ministered by the Eber to Tamasese, in the shape of uncountable German flags. The full history of this epidemic of bunting falls to be told in the next chapter. But the fact has to be chronicled here, for I believe it was to these flags that we owe the visit of the Adams, and my next and best authentic glance into a native camp. The Adams arrived in Saluafata on the 26th. On the morrow Leary and Moors landed at the village. It was still occupied by Mataafas, mostly from Manono and Savaii, few in number, high in spirit. The Tamasese pickets were meanwhile within musket range; there was maintained a steady sputtering of shots; and yet a party of Tamasese women were here on a visit to the women of Manono, with whom they sat talking and smoking, under the fire of their own relatives. It was reported that Leary took part in a council of war, and promised to join with his broadside in the next attack. It is certain he did nothing of the sort: equally certain that, in Tamasese circles, he was firmly credited with having done so. And this heightens the extraordinary character of what I have now to tell. Prudence and delicacy alike ought to have forbid the camp of Tamasese to the feet of either Leary or Moors. Moors was the original—there was a time when he had been the only—opponent of the puppet king. Leary had driven him from the seat of government; it was but a week or two since he had threatened to bombard him in his present refuge. Both were in close and daily council with his adversary, and it was no secret that Moors was supplying the latter with food. They were partisans; it lacked but a hair that they should be called belligerents; it were idle to try to deny they were the most dangerous of spies. And yet these two now sailed across the bay and landed inside the Tamasese lines at Salelesi. On the very beach they had another glimpse of the artlessness of Samoan war. Hitherto the Tamasese fleet, being hardy and unencumbered, had made a fool of the huge floating forts upon the other side; and here they were toiling, not to produce another boat on their own pattern in which they had always enjoyed the advantage, but to make a new one the type of their enemies', of which they had now proved the uselessness for months. It came on to rain as the Americans landed; and though none offered to oppose their coming ashore, none invited them to take shelter. They were nowise abashed, entered a house unbidden, and were made welcome with obvious reserve. The rain clearing off, they set forth westward, deeper into the heart of the enemies' position. Three or four young men ran some way before them, doubtless to give warning; and Leary, with his indomitable taste for mischief, kept inquiring as he went after "the high chief" Tamasese. The line of the beach was one continuous breastwork; some thirty odd iron cannon of all sizes and patterns stood mounted in embrasures; plenty grape and canister lay ready; and at every hundred yards or so the German flag was flying. The numbers of the guns and flags I give as I received them, though they test my faith. At the house of Brandeis—a little, weatherboard house, crammed at the time with natives, men, women, and squalling children—Leary and Moors again asked for "the high chief," and, were again assured that he was farther on. A little beyond, the road ran in one place somewhat inland, the two Americans had gone down to the line of the beach to continue their inspection of the breastwork, when Brandeis himself, in his shirt-sleeves and accompanied by several German officers, passed them by the line of the road. The two parties saluted in silence. Beyond Eva Point there was an observable change for the worse in the reception of the Americans; some whom they met began to mutter at Moors; and the adventurers, with tardy but commendable prudence, desisted from their search after the high chief, and began to retrace their steps. On the return, Suatele and some chiefs were drinking kava in a "big house," and called them in to join—their only invitation. But the night was closing, the rain had begun again: they stayed but for civility, and returned on board the Adams, wet and hungry, and I believe delighted with their expedition. It was perhaps the last as it was certainly one of the most extreme examples of that divinity which once hedged the white in Samoa. The feeling was already different in the camp of Mataafa, where the safety of a German loiterer had been a matter of extreme concern. Ten days later, three commissioners, an Englishman, an American, and a German, approached a post of Mataafas, were challenged by an old man with a gun, and mentioned in answer what they were. "Ifea Siamani? Which is the German?" cried the old gentleman, dancing, and with his finger on the trigger; and the commissioners stood somewhile in a very anxious posture, till they were released by the opportune arrival of a chief. It was November the 27th when Leary and Moors completed their absurd excursion; in about three weeks an event was to befall which changed at once, and probably for ever, the relations of the natives and the whites.

By the 28th Tamasese had collected seventeen hundred men in the trenches before Saluafata, thinking to attack next day. But the Mataafas evacuated the place in the night. At half-past five on the morning of the 29th a signal-gun was fired in the trenches at Laulii, and the Tamasese citadel was assaulted and defended with a fury new among Samoans. When the battle ended on the following day, one or more outworks remained in the possession of Mataafa. Another had been taken and lost as many as four times. Carried originally by a mixed force from Savaii and Tuamasanga, the victors, instead of completing fresh defences or pursuing their advantage, fell to eat and smoke and celebrate their victory with impromptu songs. In this humour a rally of the Tamaseses smote them, drove them out pell-mell, and tumbled them into the ravine, where many broke their heads and legs. Again the work was taken, again lost. Ammunition failed the belligerents; and they fought hand to hand in the contested fort with axes, clubs, and clubbed rifles. The sustained ardour of the engagement surprised even those who were engaged; and the butcher's bill was counted extraordinary by Samoans. On December 1st the women of either side collected the headless bodies of the dead, each easily identified by the name tattooed on his forearm. Mataafa is thought to have lost sixty killed; and the de Coetlogons' hospital received three women and forty men. The casualties on the Tamasese side cannot be accepted, but they were presumably much less.

CHAPTER VIII—AFFAIRS OF LAULII AND FANGALII

November-December 1888

For Becker I have not been able to conceal my distaste, for he seems to me both false and foolish. But of his successor, the unfortunately famous Dr. Knappe, we may think as of a good enough fellow driven distraught. Fond of Samoa and the Samoans, he thought to bring peace and enjoy popularity among the islanders; of a genial, amiable, and sanguine temper, he made no doubt but he could repair the breach with the English consul. Hope told a flattering tale. He awoke to find himself exchanging defiances with de Coetlogon, beaten in the field by Mataafa, surrounded on the spot by general exasperation, and disowned from home by his own government. The history of his administration leaves on the mind of the student a sentiment of pity scarcely mingled.

On Blacklock he did not call, and, in view of Leary's attitude, may be excused. But the English consul was in a different category. England, weary of the name of Samoa, and desirous only to see peace established, was prepared to wink hard during the process and to welcome the result of any German settlement. It was an unpardonable fault in Becker to have kicked and buffeted his ready-made allies into a state of jealousy, anger, and suspicion. Knappe set himself at once to efface these impressions, and the English officials rejoiced for the moment in the change. Between Knappe and de Coetlogon there seems to have been mutual sympathy; and, in considering the steps by which they were led at last into an attitude of mutual defiance, it must be remembered that both the men were sick,—Knappe from time to time prostrated with that formidable complaint, New Guinea fever, and de Coetlogon throughout his whole stay in the islands continually ailing.

Tamasese was still to be recognised, and, if possible, supported: such was the German policy. Two days after his arrival, accordingly, Knappe addressed to Mataafa a threatening despatch. The German plantation was suffering from the proximity of his "war-party." He must withdraw from Laulii at once, and, whithersoever he went, he must approach no German property nor so much as any village where there was a German trader. By five o'clock on the morrow, if he were not gone, Knappe would turn upon him "the attention of the man-of-war" and inflict a fine. The same evening, November 14th, Knappe went on board the Adler, which began to get up steam.

Three months before, such direct intervention on the part of Germany would have passed almost without protest; but the hour was now gone by. Becker's conduct, equally timid and rash, equally inconclusive and offensive, had forced the other nations into a strong feeling of common interest with Mataafa. Even had the German demands been moderate, de Coetlogon could not have forgotten the night of the taumualua, nor how Mataafa had relinquished, at his request, the attack upon the German quarter. Blacklock, with his driver of a captain at his elbow, was not likely to lag behind. And Mataafa having communicated Knappe's letter, the example of the Germans was on all hands exactly followed; the consuls hastened on board their respective war-ships, and these began to get up steam. About midnight, in a pouring rain, Pelly communicated to Fritze his intention to follow him and protect British interests; and Knappe replied that he would come on board the Lizard and see de Coetlogon personally. It was deep in the small hours, and de Coetlogon had been long asleep, when he was wakened to receive his colleague; but he started up with an old soldier's readiness. The conference was long. De Coetlogon protested, as he did afterwards in writing, against Knappe's claim: the Samoans were in a state of war; they had territorial rights; it was monstrous to prevent them from entering one of their own villages because a German trader kept the store; and in case property suffered, a claim for compensation was the proper remedy. Knappe argued that this was a question between Germans and Samoans, in which de Coetlogon had nothing to see; and that he must protect German property according to his instructions. To which de Coetlogon replied that he was himself in the same attitude to the property of the British; that he understood Knappe to be intending hostilities against Laulii; that Laulii was mortgaged to the MacArthurs; that its crops were accordingly British property; and that, while he was ever willing to recognise the territorial rights of the Samoans, he must prevent that property from being molested "by any other nation." "But if a

German man-of-war does it?" asked Knappe.—"We shall prevent it to the best of our ability," replied the colonel. It is to the credit of both men that this trying interview should have been conducted and concluded without heat; but Knappe must have returned to the Adler with darker anticipations.

At sunrise on the morning of the 15th, the three ships, each loaded with its consul, put to sea. It is hard to exaggerate the peril of the forenoon that followed, as they lay off Laulii. Nobody desired a collision, save perhaps the reckless Leary; but peace and war trembled in the balance; and when the Adler, at one period, lowered her gun ports, war appeared to preponderate. It proved, however, to be a last—and therefore surely an unwise—extremity. Knappe contented himself with visiting the rival kings, and the three ships returned to Apia before noon. Beyond a doubt, coming after Knappe's decisive letter of the day before, this impotent conclusion shook the credit of Germany among the natives of both sides; the Tamaseses fearing they were deserted, the Mataafas (with secret delight) hoping they were feared. And it gave an impetus to that ridiculous business which might have earned for the whole episode the name of the war of flags. British and American flags had been planted the night before, and were seen that morning flying over what they claimed about Laulii. British and American passengers, on the way up and down, pointed out from the decks of the war-ships, with generous vagueness, the boundaries of problematical estates. Ten days later, the beach of Saluafata bay fluttered (as I have told in the last chapter) with the flag of Germany. The Americans riposted with a claim to Tamasese's camp, some small part of which (says Knappe) did really belong to "an American nigger." The disease spread, the flags were multiplied, the operations of war became an egg-dance among miniature neutral territories; and though all men took a hand in these proceedings, all men in turn were struck with their absurdity. Mullan, Leary's successor, warned Knappe, in an emphatic despatch, not to squander and discredit the solemnity of that emblem which was all he had to be a defence to his own consulate. And Knappe himself, in his despatch of March 21st, 1889, castigates the practice with much sense. But this was after the tragicomic culmination had been reached, and the burnt rags of one of these too-frequently mendacious signals gone on a progress to Washington, like Cæsar's body, arousing indignation where it came. To such results are nations conducted by the patent artifices of a Becker.

The discussion of the morning, the silent menace and defiance of the voyage to Laulii, might have set the best-natured by the ears. But Knappe and de Coetlogon took their difference in excellent part. On the morrow, November 16th, they sat down together with Blacklock in conference. The English consul introduced his colleagues, who shook hands. If Knappe were dead-weighted with the inheritance of Becker, Blacklock was handicapped by reminiscences of Leary; it is the more to the credit of this inexperienced man that he should have maintained in the future so excellent an attitude of firmness and moderation, and that when the crash came, Knappe and de Coetlogon, not Knappe and Blacklock, were found to be the protagonists of the drama. The conference was futile. The English and American consuls admitted but one cure of the evils of the time: that the farce of the Tamasese monarchy should cease. It was one which the German refused to consider. And the agents separated without reaching any result, save that diplomatic relations had been restored between the States and Germany, and that all three were convinced of their fundamental differences.

Knappe and de Coetlogon were still friends; they had disputed and differed and come within a finger's breadth of war, and they were still friends. But an event was at hand which was to separate them for ever. On December 4th came the Royalist, Captain Hand, to relieve the Lizard. Pelly of course had to take his canvas from the consulate hospital; but he had in charge certain awnings belonging to the Royalist, and with these they made shift to cover the wounded, at that time (after the fight at Laulii) more than usually numerous. A lieutenant came to the consulate, and delivered (as I have received it) the following message: "Captain Hand's compliments, and he says you must get rid of these niggers at once, and he will help you to do it." Doubtless the reply was no more civil than the message. The promised "help," at least, followed promptly. A boat's crew landed and the awnings were stripped from the wounded, Hand himself standing on the colonel's verandah to direct operations. It were fruitless to discuss this passage from the humanitarian point of view, or from that of formal courtesy. The mind of the new captain was plainly not directed to these objects. But it is understood that he considered the existence of a hospital a source of irritation to Germans and a fault in policy. His own rude act proved in the result far more impolitic. The hospital had now been open some two months, and de Coetlogon was still on friendly terms with Knappe, and he and his wife were engaged to dine with him that day. By the morrow that was practically ended. For the rape of the awnings had two results: one, which was the fault of de Coetlogon, not at all of Hand, who could not have foreseen it; the other which it was his duty to have seen and prevented. The first was this: the de Coetlogons found themselves left with their wounded exposed to the inclemencies of the season; they must all be transported into the house and verandah; in the distress and pressure of this task, the dinner engagement was too long forgotten; and a note of excuse did not reach the German consulate before the table was set, and Knappe dressed to receive his visitors. The second consequence was inevitable. Captain Hand was scarce landed ere it became public (was "sofort bekannt," writes Knappe) that he and the consul were in opposition. All that had been gained by the demonstration at Laulii was thus immediately cast away; de Coetlogon's prestige was lessened; and it must be said plainly that Hand did less than nothing to restore it. Twice indeed he interfered, both times with success; and once, when his own person had been endangered, with vehemence; but during all the strange doings I have to narrate, he remained in close intimacy with the German consulate, and on one occasion may be said to have acted as its marshal. After the worst is over, after Bismarck has told Knappe that "the protests of his English colleague were grounded," that his own conduct "has not been good," and that in any dispute which may arise he "will find himself in the wrong," Knappe can still plead in his defence that Captain Hand "has always maintained friendly intercourse with the German authorities." Singular epitaph for an English sailor. In this complicity on the part of Hand we may find the reason—and I had almost said, the excuse—of much that was excessive in the bearing of the unfortunate Knappe.

On the 11th December, Mataafa received twenty-eight thousand cartridges, brought into the country in salt-beef kegs by the British ship Richmond. This not only sharpened the animosity between whites; following so closely on the German fizzle at Laulii, it raised a convulsion in the camp of Tamasese. On the 13th Brandeis addressed to Knappe his famous and fatal letter. I may not describe it as a letter of burning words, but it is plainly dictated by a burning heart. Tamasese and his chiefs, he announces, are now sick of the business, and ready to make peace with Mataafa. They began the war relying upon German help; they now see and say that "e faaalo Siamani i Peritania ma America, that Germany is subservient to England and the States." It is grimly given to be understood that the despatch is an ultimatum, and a last chance is being offered for the recreant ally to fulfil her pledge. To make it more plain, the document goes on with a kind of bilious irony: "The two German war-ships now in Samoa are here for the protection of German property alone; and when the Olga shall have arrived" [she arrived on the morrow] "the German war-ships will continue to do against the insurgents precisely as little as they have done heretofore." Plant flags, in fact.

Here was Knappe's opportunity, could he have stooped to seize it. I find it difficult to blame him that he could not. Far from being so inglorious as the treachery once contemplated by Becker, the acceptance of this ultimatum would have been still in the nature of a disgrace. Brandeis's letter, written by a German, was hard to swallow. It would have been hard to accept that solution which Knappe had so recently and so peremptorily refused to his brother consuls. And he was tempted, on the other hand, by recent changes. There was no Pelly to support de Coetlogon, who might now be disregarded. Mullan, Leary's successor, even if he were not precisely a Hand, was at least no Leary; and even if Mullan should show fight, Knappe had now three ships and could defy or sink him without danger. Many small circumstances moved him in the same direction. The looting of German plantations continued; the whole force of Mataafa was to a large extent subsisted from the crops of Vailele; and armed men were to be seen openly plundering bananas, breadfruit, and cocoa-nuts under the walls of the plantation building. On the night of the 13th the consulate stable had been broken into and a horse removed. On the 16th there was a riot in Apia between half-castes and sailors from the new ship Olga, each side claiming that the other was the worse of drink, both (for a wager) justly. The multiplication of flags and little neutral territories had, besides, begun to irritate the Samoans. The protests of German settlers had been received uncivilly. On the 16th the Mataafas had again sought to land in Saluafata bay, with the manifest intention to attack the Tamaseses, or (in other words) "to trespass on German lands, covered, as your Excellency knows, with flags." I quote from his requisition to Fritze, December 17th. Upon all these considerations, he goes on, it is necessary to bring the fighting to an end. Both parties are to be disarmed and returned to their villages—Mataafa first. And in case of any attempt upon Apia, the roads thither are to be held by a strong landing-party. Mataafa was to be disarmed first, perhaps rightly enough in his character of the last insurgent. Then was to have come the turn of Tamasese; but it does not appear the disarming would have had the same import or have been gone about in the same way. Germany was bound to Tamasese. No honest man would dream of blaming Knappe because he sought to redeem his country's word. The path he chose was doubtless that of honour, so far as honour was still left. But it proved to be the road to ruin.

Fritze, ranking German officer, is understood to have opposed the measure. His attitude earned him at the time unpopularity among his country-people on the spot, and should now redound to his credit. It is to be hoped he extended his opposition to some of the details. If it were possible to disarm Mataafa at all, it must be done rather by prestige than force. A party of blue-jackets landed in Samoan bush, and expected to hold against Samoans a multiplicity of forest paths, had their work cut out for them. And it was plain they should be landed in the light of day, with a discouraging openness, and even with parade. To sneak ashore by night was to increase the danger of resistance and to minimise the authority of the attack. The thing was a bluff, and it is impossible to bluff with stealth. Yet this was what was tried. A landing-party was to leave the Olga in Apia bay at two in the morning; the landing was to be at four on two parts of the foreshore of Vailele. At eight they were to be joined by a second landing-party from the Eber. By nine the Olgas were to be on the crest of Letongo Mountain, and the Ebers to be moving round the promontory by the seaward paths, "with measures of precaution," disarming all whom they encountered. There was to be no firing unless fired upon. At the appointed hour (or perhaps later) on the morning of the 19th, this unpromising business was put in hand, and there moved off from the Olga two boats with some fifty blue-jackets between them, and a praam or punt containing ninety,—the boats and the whole expedition under the command of Captain-Lieutenant Jaeckel, the praam under Lieutenant Spengler. The men had each forty rounds, one day's provisions, and their flasks filled.

In the meanwhile, Mataafa sympathisers about Apia were on the alert. Knappe had informed the consuls that the ships were to put to sea next day for the protection of German property; but the Tamaseses had been less discreet. "To-morrow at the hour of seven," they had cried to their adversaries, "you will know of a difficulty, and our guns shall be made good in broken bones." An accident had pointed expectation towards Apia. The wife of Le Māmea washed for the German ships—a perquisite, I suppose, for her husband's unwilling fidelity. She sent a man with linen on board the Adler, where he was surprised to see Le Māmea in person, and to be himself ordered instantly on shore. The news spread. If Māmea were brought down from Lotoanuu, others might have come at the same time. Tamasese himself and half his army might perhaps lie concealed on board the German ships. And a watch was accordingly set and warriors collected along the line of the shore. One detachment lay in some rifle-pits by the mouth of the Fuisá. They were commanded by Seumanu; and with his party, probably as the most contiguous to Apia, was the war-correspondent, John Klein. Of English birth, but naturalised American, this gentleman had been for some time representing the New York World in a very effective manner, always in the front, living in the field with the Samoans, and in all vicissitudes of weather, toiling to and fro with his despatches. His wisdom was perhaps not equal to his energy. He made himself conspicuous, going about armed to the teeth in a boat under the stars and stripes; and on one occasion, when he supposed himself fired upon by the Tamaseses, had the petulance to empty his revolver in the direction of their camp. By the light of the moon, which was then nearly down, this party observed the Olga's two boats and the praam, which they described as "almost sinking with men," the boats keeping well out towards the reef, the praam at the moment apparently heading for the shore. An extreme agitation seems to have reigned in the rifle-pits. What were the newcomers? What was their errand? Were they Germans or Tamaseses? Had they a mind to attack? The praam was hailed in Samoan and did not answer. It was proposed to fire upon her ere she drew near. And at last, whether on his own suggestion or that of Seumanu, Klein hailed her in English, and in terms of unnecessary melodrama. "Do not try to land here," he cried. "If you do, your blood will be upon your head." Spengler, who had never the least intention to touch at the Fuisá, put up the head of the praam to her true course and continued to move up the lagoon with an offing of some seventy or eighty yards. Along all the irregularities and obstructions of the beach, across the mouth of the Vaivasa, and through the startled village of Matafangatele, Seumanu, Klein, and seven or eight others raced to keep up, spreading the alarm and rousing reinforcements as they went. Presently a man on horse-back made his appearance on the opposite beach of Fangalii. Klein and the natives distinctly saw him signal with a lantern; which is the more strange, as the horseman (Captain Hufnagel, plantation manager of Vailele) had never a lantern to signal with. The praam kept in. Many men in white were seen to stand up, step overboard, and wade to shore. At the same time the eye of panic descried a breastwork of "foreign stone" (brick) upon the beach. Samoans are prepared to-day to swear to its existence, I believe conscientiously, although no such thing was ever made or ever intended in that place. The hour is doubtful. "It was the hour when the streak of dawn is seen, the hour known in the warfare of heathen times as the hour of the night attack," says the Mataafa official account. A native whom I met on the field declared it was at cock-crow. Captain Hufnagel, on the other hand, is sure it was long before the day. It was dark at least, and the moon down. Darkness made the Samoans bold; uncertainty as to the composition and purpose of the landing-party made them desperate. Fire was opened on the Germans, one of whom was here killed. The Germans returned it, and effected a lodgment on the beach; and the skirmish died again to silence. It was at this time, if not earlier, that Klein returned to Apia.

Here, then, were Spengler and the ninety men of the praam, landed on the beach in no very enviable posture, the woods in front filled with unnumbered enemies, but for the time successful. Meanwhile, Jaeckel and the boats had gone outside the reef, and were to land on the other side of the Vailele promontory, at Sunga, by the buildings of the plantation. It was Hufnagel's part to go and meet them. His way led straight into the woods and through the midst of the Samoans, who had but now ceased firing. He went in the saddle and at a foot's pace, feeling speed and concealment to be equally helpless, and that if he were to fall at all, he had best fall with dignity. Not a shot was fired at him; no effort made to arrest him on his errand. As he went, he spoke and even jested with the Samoans, and they answered in good part. One fellow was leaping, yelling, and tossing his axe in the air, after the way of an excited islander. "Faimalosi! go it!" said Hufnagel, and the fellow laughed and redoubled his exertions. As soon as the boats entered the lagoon, fire was again opened from the woods. The fifty blue-jackets jumped overboard, hove down the boats to be a shield, and dragged them towards the landing-place. In this way, their rations, and (what was more unfortunate) some of their miserable provision of forty rounds got wetted; but the men came to shore and garrisoned the plantation house without a casualty. Meanwhile the sound of the firing from Sunga immediately renewed the hostilities at Fangalii. The civilians on shore decided that Spengler must be at once guided to the house, and Haideln, the surveyor, accepted the dangerous errand. Like Hufnagel, he was suffered to pass without question through the midst of these platonic enemies. He found Spengler some way inland on a knoll, disastrously engaged, the woods around him filled with Samoans, who were continuously reinforced. In three successive charges, cheering as they ran, the blue-jackets burst through their scattered opponents, and made good their junction with Jaeckel. Four men only remained upon the field, the other wounded being helped by their comrades or dragging themselves painfully along.

The force was now concentrated in the house and its immediate patch of garden. Their rear, to the seaward, was unmolested; but on three sides they were beleaguered. On the left, the Samoans occupied and fired from some of the plantation offices. In front, a long rising crest of land in the horse-pasture commanded the house, and was lined with the assailants. And on the right, the hedge of the same paddock afforded them a dangerous cover. It was in this place that a Samoan sharpshooter was knocked over by Jaeckel with his own hand. The fire was maintained by the Samoans in the usual wasteful style. The roof was made a sieve; the balls passed clean through the house; Lieutenant Sieger, as he lay, already dying, on Hufnagel's bed, was despatched with a fresh wound. The Samoans showed themselves extremely enterprising:

pushed their lines forward, ventured beyond cover, and continually threatened to envelop the garden. Thrice, at least, it was necessary to repel them by a sally. The men were brought into the house from the rear, the front doors were thrown suddenly open, and the gallant blue-jackets issued cheering: necessary, successful, but extremely costly sorties. Neither could these be pushed far. The foes were undaunted; so soon as the sailors advanced at all deep in the horse-pasture, the Samoans began to close in upon both flanks; and the sally had to be recalled. To add to the dangers of the German situation, ammunition began to run low; and the cartridge-boxes of the wounded and the dead had been already brought into use before, at about eight o'clock, the Eber steamed into the bay. Her commander, Wallis, threw some shells into Letongo, one of which killed five men about their cooking-pot. The Samoans began immediately to withdraw; their movements were hastened by a sortie, and the remains of the landing-party brought on board. This was an unfortunate movement; it gave an irremediable air of defeat to what might have been else claimed for a moderate success. The blue-jackets numbered a hundred and forty all told; they were engaged separately and fought under the worst conditions, in the dark and among woods; their position in the house was scarce tenable; they lost in killed and wounded fifty-six,—forty per cent.; and their spirit to the end was above question. Whether we think of the poor sailor lads, always so pleasantly behaved in times of peace, or whether we call to mind the behaviour of the two civilians, Haideln and Hufnagel, we can only regret that brave men should stand to be exposed upon so poor a quarrel, or lives cast away upon an enterprise so hopeless.

News of the affair reached Apia early, and Moors, always curious of these spectacles of war, was immediately in the saddle. Near Matafangatele he met a Manono chief, whom he asked if there were any German dead. "I think there are about thirty of them knocked over," said he. "Have you taken their heads?" asked Moors. "Yes," said the chief. "Some foolish people did it, but I have stopped them. We ought not to cut off their heads when they do not cut off ours." He was asked what had been done with the heads. "Two have gone to Mataafa," he replied, "and one is buried right under where your horse is standing, in a basket wrapped in tapa." This was afterwards dug up, and I am told on native authority that, besides the three heads, two ears were taken. Moors next asked the Manono man how he came to be going away. "The man-of-war is throwing shells," said he. "When they stopped firing out of the house, we stopped firing also; so it was as well to scatter when the shells began. We could have killed all the white men. I wish they had been Tamaseses." This is an ex parte statement, and I give it for such; but the course of the affair, and in particular the adventures of Haideln and Hufnagel, testify to a surprising lack of animosity against the Germans. About the same time or but a little earlier than this conversation, the same spirit was being displayed. Hufnagel, with a party of labour, had gone out to bring in the German dead, when he was surprised to be suddenly fired on from the wood. The boys he had with him were not negritos, but Polynesians from the Gilbert Islands; and he suddenly remembered that these might be easily mistaken for a detachment of Tamaseses. Bidding his boys conceal themselves in a thicket, this brave man walked into the open. So soon as he was recognised, the firing ceased, and the labourers followed him in safety. This is chivalrous war; but there was a side to it less chivalrous. As Moors drew nearer to Vailele, he began to meet Samoans with hats, guns, and even shirts, taken from the German sailors. With one of these who had a hat and a gun he stopped and spoke. The hat was handed up for him to look at; it had the late owner's name on the inside. "Where is he?" asked Moors. "He is dead; I cut his head off." "You shot him?" "No, somebody else shot him in the hip. When I came, he put up his hands, and cried: 'Don't kill me; I am a Malietoa man.' I did not believe him, and I cut his head off...... Have you any ammunition to fit that gun?" "I do not know." "What has become of the cartridge-belt?" "Another fellow grabbed that and the cartridges, and he won't give them to me." A dreadful and silly picture of barbaric war. The words of the German sailor must be regarded as imaginary: how was the poor lad to speak native, or the Samoan to understand German? When Moors came as far as Sunga, the Eber was yet in the bay, the smoke of battle still lingered among the trees, which were themselves marked with a thousand bullet-wounds. But the affair was over, the combatants, German and Samoan, were all gone, and only a couple of negrito labour boys lurked on the scene. The village of Letongo beyond was equally silent; part of it was wrecked by the shells of the Eber, and still smoked; the inhabitants had fled. On the beach were the native boats, perhaps five thousand dollars' worth, deserted by the Mataafas and overlooked by the Germans, in their common hurry to escape. Still Moors held eastward by the sea-paths. It was his hope to get a view from the other side of the promontory, towards Laulii. In the way he found a house hidden in the wood and among rocks, where an aged and sick woman was being tended by her elderly daughter. Last lingerers in that deserted piece of coast, they seemed indifferent to the events which had thus left them solitary, and, as the daughter said, did not know where Mataafa was, nor where Tamasese.

It is the official Samoan pretension that the Germans fired first at Fangalii. In view of all German and some native testimony, the text of Fritze's orders, and the probabilities of the case, no honest mind will believe it for a moment. Certainly the Samoans fired first. As certainly they were betrayed into the engagement in the agitation of the moment, and it was not till afterwards that they understood what they had done. Then, indeed, all Samoa drew a breath of wonder and delight. The invincible had fallen; the men of the vaunted war-ships had been met in the field by the braves of Mataafa: a superstition was no more. Conceive this people steadily as schoolboys; and conceive the elation in any school if the head boy should suddenly arise and drive the rector from the schoolhouse. I have received one instance of the feeling instantly aroused. There lay at the time in the consular hospital an old chief who was a pet of the colonel's. News reached him of the glorious event; he was sick, he thought himself sinking, sent for the colonel, and gave him his gun. "Don't let the Germans get it," said the old gentleman, and having received a promise, was at peace.

CHAPTER IX—"FUROR CONSULARIS"

December 1888 *to March* 1889

Knappe, in the Adler, with a flag of truce at the fore, was entering Laulii Bay when the Eber brought him the news of the night's reverse. His heart was doubtless wrung for his young countrymen who had been butchered and mutilated in the dark woods, or now lay suffering, and some of them dying, on the ship. And he must have been startled as he recognised his own position. He had gone too far; he had stumbled into war, and, what was worse, into defeat; he had thrown away German lives for less than nothing, and now saw himself condemned either to accept defeat, or to kick and pummel his failure into something like success; either to accept defeat, or take frenzy for a counsellor. Yesterday, in cold blood, he had judged it necessary to have the woods to the westward guarded lest the evacuation of Laulii should prove only the peril of Apia. To-day, in the irritation and alarm of failure, he forgot or despised his previous reasoning, and, though his detachment was beat back to the ships, proceeded with the remainder of his maimed design. The only change he made was to haul down the flag of truce. He had now no wish to meet with Mataafa. Words were out of season, shells must speak.

At this moment an incident befell him which must have been trying to his self-command. The new American ship Nipsic entered Laulii Bay; her commander, Mullan, boarded the Adler to protest, succeeded in wresting from Knappe a period of delay in order that the women might be spared, and sent a lieutenant to Mataafa with a warning. The camp was already excited by the news and the trophies of Fangalii. Already Tamasese and Lotoanuu seemed secondary objectives to the Germans and Apia. Mullan's message put an end to hesitation. Laulii was evacuated. The troops streamed westward by the mountain side, and took up the same day a strong position about Tanungamanono and Mangiangi, some two miles behind Apia, which they threatened with the one hand, while with the other they continued to draw their supplies from the devoted plantations of the German firm. Laulii, when it was shelled, was empty. The British flags were, of course, fired upon; and I hear that one of them was struck down, but I think every one must be privately of the mind that it was fired upon and fell, in a place where it had little business to be shown.

Such was the military epilogue to the ill-judged adventure of Fangalii; it was difficult for failure to be more complete. But the other consequences were of a darker colour and brought the whites immediately face to face in a spirit of ill-favoured animosity. Knappe was mourning the defeat and death of his country-folk, he was standing aghast over the ruin of his own career, when Mullan boarded him. The successor of Leary served himself, in that bitter moment, heir to Leary's part. And in Mullan, Knappe saw more even than the successor of Leary,—he saw in him the representative of Klein. Klein had hailed the praam from the rifle-pits; he had there uttered ill-chosen words, unhappily prophetic; it is even likely that he was present at the time of the first fire. To accuse him of the design and conduct of the whole attack was but a step forward; his own vapouring served to corroborate the accusation; and it was not long before the German consulate was in possession of sworn native testimony in support. The worth of native testimony is small, the worth of white testimony not overwhelming; and I am in the painful position of not being able to subscribe either to Klein's own account of the affair or to that of his accusers. Klein was extremely flurried; his interest as a reporter must have tempted him at first to make the most of his share in the exploit, the immediate peril in which he soon found himself to stand must have at least suggested to him the idea of minimising it; one way and another, he is not a good witness. As for the natives, they were no doubt cross-examined in that hall of terror, the German consulate, where they might be trusted to lie like schoolboys, or (if the reader prefer it) like Samoans. By outside white testimony, it remains established for me that Klein returned to Apia either before or immediately after the first shots. That he ever sought or was ever allowed a share in the command may be denied peremptorily; but it is more than likely that he expressed himself in an excited manner and with a highly inflammatory effect upon his hearers. He was, at least, severely punished. The Germans, enraged by his provocative behaviour and what they thought to be his German birth, demanded him to be tried before court-

112

martial; he had to skulk inside the sentries of the American consulate, to be smuggled on board a war-ship, and to be carried almost by stealth out of the island; and what with the agitations of his mind, and the results of a marsh fever contracted in the lines of Mataafa, reached Honolulu a very proper object of commiseration. Nor was Klein the only accused: de Coetlogon was himself involved. As the boats passed Matautu, Knappe declares a signal was made from the British consulate. Perhaps we should rather read "from its neighbourhood"; since, in the general warding of the coast, the point of Matautu could scarce have been neglected. On the other hand, there is no doubt that the Samoans, in the anxiety of that night of watching and fighting, crowded to the friendly consul for advice. Late in the night, the wounded Siteoni, lying on the colonel's verandah, one corner of which had been blinded down that he might sleep, heard the coming and going of bare feet and the voices of eager consultation. And long after, a man who had been discharged from the colonel's employment took upon himself to swear an affidavit as to the nature of the advice then given, and to carry the document to the German consul. It was an act of private revenge; it fell long out of date in the good days of Dr. Stuebel, and had no result but to discredit the gentleman who volunteered it. Colonel de Coetlogon had his faults, but they did not touch his honour; his bare word would always outweigh a waggon-load of such denunciations; and he declares his behaviour on that night to have been blameless. The question was besides inquired into on the spot by Sir John Thurston, and the colonel honourably acquitted. But during the weeks that were now to follow, Knappe believed the contrary; he believed not only that Moors and others had supplied ammunition and Klein commanded in the field, but that de Coetlogon had made the signal of attack; that though his blue-jackets had bled and fallen against the arms of Samoans, these were supplied, inspired, and marshalled by Americans and English.

The legend was the more easily believed because it embraced and was founded upon so much truth. Germans lay dead, the German wounded groaned in their cots; and the cartridges by which they fell had been sold by an American and brought into the country in a British bottom. Had the transaction been entirely mercenary, it would already have been hard to swallow; but it was notoriously not so. British and Americans were notoriously the partisans of Mataafa. They rejoiced in the result of Fangalii, and so far from seeking to conceal their rejoicing, paraded and displayed it. Calumny ran high. Before the dead were buried, while the wounded yet lay in pain and fever, cowardly accusations of cowardice were levelled at the German blue-jackets. It was said they had broken and run before their enemies, and that they had huddled helpless like sheep in the plantation house. Small wonder if they had; small wonder had they been utterly destroyed. But the fact was heroically otherwise; and these dastard calumnies cut to the blood. They are not forgotten; perhaps they will never be forgiven.

In the meanwhile, events were pressing towards a still more trenchant opposition. On the 20th, the three consuls met and parted without agreement, Knappe announcing that he had lost men and must take the matter in his own hands to avenge their death. On the 21st the Olga came before Matafangatele, ordered the delivery of all arms within the hour, and at the end of that period, none being brought, shelled and burned the village. The shells fell for the most part innocuous; an eyewitness saw children at play beside the flaming houses; not a soul was injured; and the one noteworthy event was the mutilation of Captain Hamilton's American flag. In one sense an incident too small to be chronicled, in another this was of historic interest and import. These rags of tattered bunting occasioned the display of a new sentiment in the United States; and the republic of the West, hitherto so apathetic and unwieldy, but already stung by German nonchalance, leaped to its feet for the first time at the news of this fresh insult. As though to make the inefficiency of the war-ships more apparent, three shells were thrown inland at Mangiangi; they flew high over the Mataafa camp, where the natives could "hear them singing" as they flew, and fell behind in the deep romantic valley of the Vaisingano. Mataafa had been already summoned on board the Adler; his life promised if he came, declared "in danger" if he came not; and he had declined in silence the unattractive invitation. These fresh hostile acts showed him that the worst had come. He was in strength, his force posted along the whole front of the mountain behind Apia, Matautu occupied, the Siumu road lined up to the houses of the town with warriors passionate for war. The occasion was unique, and there is no doubt that he designed to seize it. The same day of this bombardment, he sent word bidding all English and Americans wear a black band upon their arm, so that his men should recognise and spare them. The hint was taken, and the band worn for a continuance of days. To have refused would have been insane; but to consent was unhappily to feed the resentment of the Germans by a fresh sign of intelligence with their enemies, and to widen the breach between the races by a fresh and a scarce pardonable mark of their division. The same day again the Germans repeated one of their earlier offences by firing on a boat within the harbour. Times were changed; they were now at war and in peril, the rigour of military advantage might well be seized by them and pardoned by others; but it so chanced that the bullets flew about the ears of Captain Hand, and that commander is said to have been insatiable of apologies. The affair, besides, had a deplorable effect on the inhabitants. A black band (they saw) might protect them from the Mataafas, not from undiscriminating shots. Panic ensued. The war-ships were open to receive the fugitives, and the gentlemen who had made merry over Fangalii were seen to thrust each other from the wharves in their eagerness to flee Apia. I willingly drop the curtain on the shameful picture.

Meanwhile, on the German side of the bay, a more manly spirit was exhibited in circumstances of alarming weakness. The plantation managers and overseers had all retreated to Matafele, only one (I understand) remaining at his post. The whole German colony was thus collected in one spot, and could count and wonder at its scanty numbers. Knappe declares (to my surprise) that the war-ships could not spare him more than fifty men a day. The great extension of the German quarter, he goes on, did not "allow a full occupation of the outer line"; hence they had shrunk into the western end by the firm buildings, and the inhabitants were warned to fall back on this position, in the case of an alert. So that he who had set forth, a day or so before, to disarm the Mataafas in the open field, now found his resources scarce adequate to garrison the buildings of the firm. But Knappe seemed unteachable by fate. It is probable he thought he had

"Already waded in so deep,

Returning were as tedious as go o'er";

it is certain that he continued, on the scene of his defeat and in the midst of his weakness, to bluster and menace like a conqueror. Active war, which he lacked the means of attempting, was continually threatened. On the 22nd he sought the aid of his brother consuls to maintain the neutral territory against Mataafa; and at the same time, as though meditating instant deeds of prowess, refused to be bound by it himself. This singular proposition was of course refused: Blacklock remarking that he had no fear of the natives, if these were let alone; de Coetlogon refusing in the circumstances to recognise any neutral territory at all. In vain Knappe amended and baited his proposal with the offer of forty-eight or ninety-six hours' notice, according as his objective should be near or within the boundary of the Eleele Sa. It was rejected; and he learned that he must accept war with all its consequences—and not that which he desired—war with the immunities of peace.

This monstrous exigence illustrates the man's frame of mind. It has been still further illuminated in the German white-book by printing alongside of his despatches those of the unimpassioned Fritze. On January 8th the consulate was destroyed by fire. Knappe says it was the work of incendiaries, "without doubt"; Fritze admits that "everything seems to show" it was an accident. "Tamasese's people fit to bear arms," writes Knappe, "are certainly for the moment equal to Mataafa's," though restrained from battle by the lack of ammunition. "As for Tamasese," says Fritze of the same date, "he is now but a phantom—dient er nur als Gespenst. His party, for practical purposes, is no longer large. They pretend ammunition to be lacking, but what they lack most is good-will. Captain Brandeis, whose influence is now small, declares they can no longer sustain a serious engagement, and is himself in the intention of leaving Samoa by the Lübeck of the 5th February." And Knappe, in the same despatch, confutes himself and confirms the testimony of his naval colleague, by the admission that "the re-establishment of Tamasese's government is, under present circumstances, not to be thought of." Plainly, then, he was not so much seeking to deceive others, as he was himself possessed; and we must regard the whole series of his acts and despatches as the agitations of a fever.

The British steamer Richmond returned to Apia, January 15th. On the last voyage she had brought the ammunition already so frequently referred to; as a matter of fact, she was again bringing contraband of war. It is necessary to be explicit upon this, which served as spark to so great a flame of scandal. Knappe was justified in interfering; he would have been worthy of all condemnation if he had neglected, in his posture of semi-investment, a precaution so elementary; and the manner in which he set about attempting it was conciliatory and almost timid. He applied to Captain Hand, and begged him to accept himself the duty of "controlling" the discharge of the Richmond's cargo. Hand was unable to move without his consul; and at night an armed boat from the Germans boarded, searched, and kept possession of, the suspected ship. The next day, as by an after-thought, war and martial law were proclaimed for the Samoan Islands, the introduction of contraband of war forbidden, and ships and boats declared liable to search. "All support of the rebels will be punished by martial law," continued the proclamation, "no matter to what nationality the person [Thäter] may belong."

Hand, it has been seen, declined to act in the matter of the Richmond without the concurrence of his consul; but I have found no evidence that either Hand or Knappe communicated with de Coetlogon, with whom they were both at daggers drawn. First the seizure and next the proclamation seem to have burst on the English consul from a clear sky; and he wrote on the same day, throwing doubt on Knappe's authority to declare war. Knappe replied on the 20th that the Imperial German Government had been at war as a matter of fact since December 19th, and that it was only for the convenience of the subjects of other states that he had been empowered to make a formal declaration. "From that moment," he added, "martial law prevails in Samoa." De Coetlogon instantly retorted, declining martial law for British subjects, and announcing a proclamation in that sense. Instantly, again, came that astonishing document, Knappe's rejoinder, without pause, without reflection—the pens screeching on the paper, the messengers (you would think) running from consulate to consulate: "I have had the honour to receive your Excellency's [Hochwohlgeboren] agreeable communication of to-day. Since, on the ground of received instructions, martial law has been declared in Samoa, British subjects as well as others fall under its application. I warn you therefore to abstain from such a proclamation as you announce in your letter. It will be such a piece of business as shall make yourself answerable

117

under martial law. Besides, your proclamation will be disregarded." De Coetlogon of course issued his proclamation at once, Knappe retorted with another, and night closed on the first stage of this insane collision. I hear the German consul was on this day prostrated with fever; charity at least must suppose him hardly answerable for his language.

Early on the 21st, Mr. Mansfield Gallien, a passing traveller, was seized in his berth on board the Richmond, and carried, half-dressed, on board a German war-ship. His offence was, in the circumstances and after the proclamation, substantial. He had gone the day before, in the spirit of a tourist to Mataafa's camp, had spoken with the king, and had even recommended him an appeal to Sir George Grey. Fritze, I gather, had been long uneasy; this arrest on board a British ship fitted the measure. Doubtless, as he had written long before, the consul alone was responsible "on the legal side"; but the captain began to ask himself, "What next?"—telegraphed direct home for instructions, "Is arrest of foreigners on foreign vessels legal?"—and was ready, at a word from Captain Hand, to discharge his dangerous prisoner. The word in question (so the story goes) was not without a kind of wit. "I wish you would set that man ashore," Hand is reported to have said, indicating Gallien; "I wish you would set that man ashore, to save me the trouble." The same day de Coetlogon published a proclamation requesting captains to submit to search for contraband of war.

On the 22nd the Samoa Times and South Sea Advertiser was suppressed by order of Fritze. I have hitherto refrained from mentioning the single paper of our islands, that I might deal with it once for all. It is of course a tiny sheet; but I have often had occasion to wonder at the ability of its articles, and almost always at the decency of its tone. Officials may at times be a little roughly, and at times a little captiously, criticised; private persons are habitually respected; and there are many papers in England, and still more in the States, even of leading organs in chief cities, that might envy, and would do well to imitate, the courtesy and discretion of the Samoa Times. Yet the editor, Cusack, is only an amateur in journalism, and a carpenter by trade. His chief fault is one perhaps inevitable in so small a place—that he seems a little in the leading of a clique; but his interest in the public weal is genuine and generous. One man's meat is another man's poison: Anglo-Saxons and Germans have been differently brought up. To our galled experience the paper appears moderate; to their untried sensations it seems violent. We think a public man fair game; we think it a part of his duty, and I am told he finds it a part of his reward, to be continually canvassed by the press. For the Germans, on the other hand, an official wears a certain sacredness; when he is called over the coals, they are shocked, and (if the official be a German) feel that Germany itself has been insulted. The Samoa Times had been long a mountain of offence. Brandeis had imported from the colonies another printer of the name of Jones, to deprive Cusack of the government printing. German sailors had come ashore one day, wild with offended patriotism, to punish the editor with stripes, and the result was delightfully amusing. The champions asked for the English printer. They were shown the wrong man, and the blows intended for Cusack had hailed on the shoulders of his rival Jones. On the 12th, Cusack had reprinted an article from a San Francisco paper; the Germans had complained; and de Coetlogon, in a moment of weakness, had fined the editor twenty pounds. The judgment was afterwards reversed in Fiji; but even at the time it had not satisfied the Germans. And so now, on the third day of martial law, the paper was suppressed. Here we have another of these international obscurities. To Fritze the step seemed natural and obvious; for Anglo-Saxons it was a hand laid upon the altar; and the month was scarce out before the voice of Senator Frye announced to his colleagues that free speech had been suppressed in Samoa.

Perhaps we must seek some similar explanation for Fritze's short-lived code, published and withdrawn the next day, the 23rd. Fritze himself was in no humour for extremities. He was much in the position of a lieutenant who should perceive his captain urging the ship upon the rocks. It is plain he had lost all confidence in his commanding officer "upon the legal side"; and we find him writing home with anxious candour. He had understood that martial law implied military possession; he was in military possession of nothing but his ship, and shrewdly suspected that his martial jurisdiction should be confined within the same limits. "As a matter of fact," he writes, "we do not occupy the territory, and cannot give foreigners the necessary protection, because Mataafa and his people can at any moment forcibly

119

interrupt me in my jurisdiction." Yet in the eyes of Anglo-Saxons the severity of his code appeared burlesque. I give but three of its provisions. The crime of inciting German troops "by any means, as, for instance, informing them of proclamations by the enemy," was punishable with death; that of "publishing or secretly distributing anything, whether printed or written, bearing on the war," with prison or deportation; and that of calling or attending a public meeting, unless permitted, with the same. Such were the tender mercies of Knappe, lurking in the western end of the German quarter, where Mataafa could "at any moment" interrupt his jurisdiction.

On the 22nd (day of the suppression of the Times) de Coetlogon wrote to inquire if hostilities were intended against Great Britain, which Knappe on the same day denied. On the 23rd de Coetlogon sent a complaint of hostile acts, such as the armed and forcible entry of the Richmond before the declaration and arrest of Gallien. In his reply, dated the 24th, Knappe took occasion to repeat, although now with more self-command, his former threat against de Coetlogon. "I am still of the opinion," he writes, "that even foreign consuls are liable to the application of martial law, if they are guilty of offences against the belligerent state." The same day (24th) de Coetlogon complained that Fletcher, manager for Messrs. MacArthur, had been summoned by Fritze. In answer, Knappe had "the honour to inform your Excellency that since the declaration of the state of war, British subjects are liable to martial law, and Mr. Fletcher will be arrested if he does not appear." Here, then, was the gauntlet thrown down, and de Coetlogon was burning to accept it. Fletcher's offence was this. Upon the 22nd a steamer had come in from Wellington, specially chartered to bring German despatches to Apia. The rumour came along with her from New Zealand that in these despatches Knappe would find himself rebuked, and Fletcher was accused of having "interested himself in the spreading of this rumour." His arrest was actually ordered, when Hand succeeded in persuading him to surrender. At the German court, the case was dismissed "wegen Nichtigkeit"; and the acute stage of these distempers may be said to have ended. Blessed are the peacemakers. Hand had perhaps averted a collision. What is more certain, he had offered to the world a perfectly original reading of the part of British seaman.

Hand may have averted a collision, I say; but I am tempted to believe otherwise. I am tempted to believe the threat to arrest Fletcher was the last mutter of the declining tempest and a mere sop to Knappe's self-respect. I am tempted to believe the rumour in question was substantially correct, and the steamer from Wellington had really brought the German consul grounds for hesitation, if not orders to retreat. I believe the unhappy man to have awakened from a dream, and to have read ominous writing on the wall. An enthusiastic popularity surrounded him among the Germans. It was natural. Consul and colony had passed through an hour of serious peril, and the consul had set the example of undaunted courage. He was entertained at dinner. Fritze, who was known to have secretly opposed him, was scorned and avoided. But the clerks of the German firm were one thing, Prince Bismarck was another; and on a cold review of these events, it is not improbable that Knappe may have envied the position of his naval colleague. It is certain, at least, that he set himself to shuffle and capitulate; and when the blow fell, he was able to reply that the martial law business had in the meanwhile come right; that the English and American consular courts stood open for ordinary cases and that in different conversations with Captain Hand, "who has always maintained friendly intercourse with the German authorities," it had been repeatedly explained that only the supply of weapons and ammunition, or similar aid and support, was to come under German martial law. Was it weapons or ammunition that Fletcher had supplied? But it is unfair to criticise these wrigglings of an unfortunate in a false position.

In a despatch of the 23rd, which has not been printed, Knappe had told his story: how he had declared war, subjected foreigners to martial law, and been received with a counter-proclamation by the English consul; and how (in an interview with Mataafa chiefs at the plantation house of Motuotua, of which I cannot find the date) he had demanded the cession of arms and of ringleaders for punishment, and proposed to assume the government of the islands. On February 12th he received Bismarck's answer: "You had no right to take foreigners from the jurisdiction of their consuls. The protest of your English colleague is grounded. In disputes which may arise from this cause you will find yourself in the wrong. The demand formulated by you, as to the assumption of the government of Samoa by Germany, lay outside of your instructions and of our design. Take it immediately back. If your telegram is here rightly understood, I cannot call your conduct good." It must be a hard heart that does not sympathise with Knappe in the hour when he received this document. Yet it may be said that his troubles were still in the beginning. Men had contended against him, and he had not prevailed; he was now to be at war with the elements, and find his name identified with an immense disaster.

One more date, however, must be given first. It was on February 27th that Fritze formally announced martial law to be suspended, and himself to have relinquished the control of the police.

CHAPTER X—THE HURRICANE

March 1889

The so-called harbour of Apia is formed in part by a recess of the coast-line at Matautu, in part by the slim peninsula of Mulinuu, and in part by the fresh waters of the Mulivai and Vaisingano. The barrier reef—that singular breakwater that makes so much of the circuit of Pacific islands—is carried far to sea at Matautu and Mulinuu; inside of these two horns it runs sharply landward, and between them it is burst or dissolved by the fresh water. The shape of the enclosed anchorage may be compared to a high-shouldered jar or bottle with a funnel mouth. Its sides are almost everywhere of coral; for the reef not only bounds it to seaward and forms the neck and mouth, but skirting about the beach, it forms the bottom also. As in the bottle of commerce, the bottom is re-entrant, and the shore-reef runs prominently forth into the basin and makes a dangerous cape opposite the fairway of the entrance. Danger is, therefore, on all hands. The entrance gapes three cables wide at the narrowest, and the formidable surf of the Pacific thunders both outside and in. There are days when speech is difficult in the chambers of shore-side houses; days when no boat can land, and when men are broken by stroke of sea against the wharves. As I write these words, three miles in the mountains, and with the land-breeze still blowing from the island summit, the sound of that vexed harbour hums in my ears. Such a creek in my native coast of Scotland would scarce be dignified with the mark of an anchor in the chart; but in the favoured climate of Samoa, and with the mechanical regularity of the winds in the Pacific, it forms, for ten or eleven months out of the twelve, a safe if hardly a commodious port. The ill-found island traders ride there with their insufficient moorings the year through, and discharge, and are loaded, without apprehension. Of danger, when it comes, the glass gives timely warning; and that any modern war-ship, furnished with the power of steam, should have been lost in Apia, belongs not so much to nautical as to political history.

The weather throughout all that winter (the turbulent summer of the islands) was unusually fine, and the circumstance had been commented on as providential, when so many Samoans were lying on their weapons in the bush. By February it began to break in occasional gales. On February 10th a German brigantine was driven ashore. On the 14th the same misfortune befell an American brigantine and a schooner. On both these days, and again on the 7th March, the men-of-war must steam to their anchors. And it was in this last month, the most dangerous of the twelve, that man's animosities crowded that indentation of the reef with costly, populous, and vulnerable ships.

I have shown, perhaps already at too great a length, how violently passion ran upon the spot; how high this series of blunders and mishaps had heated the resentment of the Germans against all other nationalities and of all other nationalities against the Germans. But there was one country beyond the borders of Samoa where the question had aroused a scarce less angry sentiment. The breach of the Washington Congress, the evidence of Sewall before a sub-committee on foreign relations, the proposal to try Klein before a military court, and the rags of Captain Hamilton's flag, had combined to stir the people of the States to an unwonted fervour. Germany was for the time the abhorred of nations. Germans in America publicly disowned the country of their birth. In Honolulu, so near the scene of action, German and American young men fell to blows in the street. In the same city, from no traceable source, and upon no possible authority, there arose a rumour of tragic news to arrive by the next occasion, that the Nipsic had opened fire on the Adler, and the Adler had sunk her on the first reply. Punctually on the day appointed, the news came; and the two nations, instead of being plunged into war, could only mingle tears over the loss of heroes.

By the second week in March three American ships were in Apia bay,— the Nipsic, the Vandalia, and the Trenton, carrying the flag of Rear-Admiral Kimberley; three German,—the Adler, the Eber, and the Olga; and one British,—the Calliope, Captain Kane. Six merchant-men, ranging from twenty-five up to five hundred tons, and a number of small craft, further encumbered the anchorage. Its capacity is estimated by Captain Kane at four large ships; and the latest arrivals, the Vandalia and Trenton, were in consequence excluded, and lay without in the passage. Of the seven war-ships, the seaworthiness of two was questionable: the Trenton's, from an original defect in her construction, often reported, never remedied—her hawse-pipes leading in on the berth-deck; the Eber's, from an injury to her screw in the blow of February 14th. In this overcrowding of ships in an open entry of the reef, even the eye of the landsman could spy danger; and Captain-Lieutenant Wallis of the Eber openly blamed and lamented, not many hours before the catastrophe, their helpless posture. Temper once more triumphed. The army of Mataafa still hung imminent behind the town; the German quarter was still daily garrisoned with fifty sailors from the squadron; what was yet more influential, Germany and the States, at least in Apia bay, were on the brink of war, viewed each other with looks of hatred, and scarce observed the letter of civility. On the day of the admiral's arrival, Knappe failed to call on him, and on the morrow called on him while he was on shore. The slight was remarked and resented, and the two squadrons clung more obstinately to their dangerous station.

On the 15th the barometer fell to 29.11 in. by 2 P.M. This was the moment when every sail in port should have escaped. Kimberley, who flew the only broad pennant, should certainly have led the way: he clung, instead, to his moorings, and the Germans doggedly followed his example: semi-belligerents, daring each other and the violence of heaven. Kane, less immediately involved, was led in error by the report of residents and a fallacious rise in the glass; he stayed with the others, a misjudgment that was like to cost him dear. All were moored, as is the custom in Apia, with two anchors practically east and west, clear hawse to the north, and a kedge astern. Topmasts were struck, and the ships made snug. The night closed black, with sheets of rain. By midnight it blew a gale; and by the morning watch, a tempest. Through what remained of darkness, the captains impatiently expected day, doubtful if they were dragging, steaming gingerly to their moorings, and afraid to steam too much.

Day came about six, and presented to those on shore a seizing and terrific spectacle. In the pressure of the squalls the bay was obscured as if by midnight, but between them a great part of it was clearly if darkly visible

125

amid driving mist and rain. The wind blew into the harbour mouth. Naval authorities describe it as of hurricane force. It had, however, few or none of the effects on shore suggested by that ominous word, and was successfully withstood by trees and buildings. The agitation of the sea, on the other hand, surpassed experience and description. Seas that might have awakened surprise and terror in the midst of the Atlantic ranged bodily and (it seemed to observers) almost without diminution into the belly of that flask-shaped harbour; and the war-ships were alternately buried from view in the trough, or seen standing on end against the breast of billows.

The Trenton at daylight still maintained her position in the neck of the bottle. But five of the remaining ships tossed, already close to the bottom, in a perilous and helpless crowd; threatening ruin to each other as they tossed; threatened with a common and imminent destruction on the reefs. Three had been already in collision: the Olga was injured in the quarter, the Adler had lost her bowsprit; the Nipsic had lost her smoke-stack, and was making steam with difficulty, maintaining her fire with barrels of pork, and the smoke and sparks pouring along the level of the deck. For the seventh war-ship the day had come too late; the Eber had finished her last cruise; she was to be seen no more save by the eyes of divers. A coral reef is not only an instrument of destruction, but a place of sepulchre; the submarine cliff is profoundly undercut, and presents the mouth of a huge antre in which the bodies of men and the hulls of ships are alike hurled down and buried. The Eber had dragged anchors with the rest; her injured screw disabled her from steaming vigorously up; and a little before day she had struck the front of the coral, come off, struck again, and gone down stern foremost, oversetting as she went, into the gaping hollow of the reef. Of her whole complement of nearly eighty, four souls were cast alive on the beach; and the bodies of the remainder were, by the voluminous outpouring of the flooded streams, scoured at last from the harbour, and strewed naked on the seaboard of the island.

Five ships were immediately menaced with the same destruction. The Eber vanished—the four poor survivors on shore—read a dreadful commentary on their danger; which was swelled out of all proportion by the violence of their own movements as they leaped and fell among the billows.

By seven the Nipsic was so fortunate as to avoid the reef and beach upon a space of sand; where she was immediately deserted by her crew, with the assistance of Samoans, not without loss of life. By about eight it was the turn of the Adler. She was close down upon the reef; doomed herself, it might yet be possible to save a portion of her crew; and for this end Captain Fritze placed his reliance on the very hugeness of the seas that threatened him. The moment was watched for with the anxiety of despair, but the coolness of disciplined courage. As she rose on the fatal wave, her moorings were simultaneously slipped; she broached to in rising; and the sea heaved her bodily upward and cast her down with a concussion on the summit of the reef, where she lay on her beam-ends, her back broken, buried in breaching seas, but safe. Conceive a table: the Eber in the darkness had been smashed against the rim and flung below; the Adler, cast free in the nick of opportunity, had been thrown upon the top. Many were injured in the concussion; many tossed into the water; twenty perished. The survivors crept again on board their ship, as it now lay, and as it still remains, keel to the waves, a monument of the sea's potency. In still weather, under a cloudless sky, in those seasons when that ill-named ocean, the Pacific, suffers its vexed shores to rest, she lies high and dry, the spray scarce touching her—the hugest structure of man's hands within a circuit of a thousand miles—tossed up there like a schoolboy's cap upon a shelf; broken like an egg; a thing to dream of.

The unfriendly consuls of Germany and Britain were both that morning in Matautu, and both displayed their nobler qualities. De Coetlogon, the grim old soldier, collected his family and kneeled with them in an agony of prayer for those exposed. Knappe, more fortunate in that he was called to a more active service, must, upon the striking of the Adler, pass to his own consulate. From this he was divided by the Vaisingano, now a raging torrent, impetuously charioting the trunks of trees. A kelpie might have dreaded to attempt the passage; we may conceive this brave but unfortunate and now ruined man to have found a natural joy in the exposure of his life; and twice that day, coming and going, he braved the fury of the river. It was possible, in spite of the darkness of the hurricane and the continual breaching of the seas, to remark human movements on the Adler; and by the help of Samoans, always nobly forward in the work, whether for friend or enemy, Knappe sought long to get a line conveyed from shore, and was for long defeated. The shore guard of fifty men stood to their arms the while upon the beach, useless themselves, and a great deterrent of Samoan usefulness. It was perhaps impossible that this mistake should be avoided. What more natural, to the mind of a European, than that the Mataafas should fall upon the Germans in this hour of their disadvantage? But they had no other thought than to assist; and those who now rallied beside Knappe braved (as they supposed) in doing so a double danger, from the fury of the sea and the weapons of their enemies. About nine, a quarter-master swam ashore, and reported all the officers and some sixty men alive but in pitiable case; some with broken limbs, others insensible from the drenching of the breakers. Later in the forenoon, certain valorous Samoans succeeded in reaching the wreck and returning with a line; but it was speedily broken; and all subsequent attempts proved unavailing, the strongest adventurers being cast back again by the bursting seas. Thenceforth, all through that day and night, the deafened survivors must continue to endure their martyrdom; and one officer died, it was supposed from agony of mind, in his inverted cabin.

Three ships still hung on the next margin of destruction, steaming desperately to their moorings, dashed helplessly together. The Calliope was the nearest in; she had the Vandalia close on her port side and a little ahead, the Olga close a-starboard, the reef under her heel; and steaming and veering on her cables, the unhappy ship fenced with her three dangers. About a quarter to nine she carried away the Vandalia's quarter gallery with her jib-boom; a moment later, the Olga had near rammed her from the other side. By nine the Vandalia dropped down on her too fast to be avoided, and clapped her stern under the bowsprit of the English ship, the fastenings of which were burst asunder as she rose. To avoid cutting her down, it was necessary for the Calliope to stop and even to reverse her engines; and her rudder was at the moment—or it seemed so to the eyes of those on board—within ten feet of the reef. "Between the Vandalia and the reef" (writes Kane, in his excellent report) "it was destruction." To repeat Fritze's manoeuvre with the Adler was impossible; the Calliope was too heavy. The one possibility of escape was to go out. If the engines should stand, if they should have power to drive the ship against wind and sea, if she should answer the helm, if the wheel, rudder, and gear should hold out, and if they were favoured with a clear blink of weather in which to see and avoid the outer reef—there, and there only, were safety. Upon this catalogue of "ifs" Kane staked his all. He signalled to the engineer for every pound of steam—and at that moment (I am told) much of the machinery was already red-hot. The ship was sheered well to starboard of the Vandalia, the last remaining cable slipped. For a time—and there was no onlooker so cold-blooded as to offer a guess at its duration—the Calliope lay stationary; then gradually drew ahead. The highest speed claimed for her that day is of one sea-mile an hour. The question of times and seasons, throughout all this roaring business, is obscured by a dozen contradictions; I have but chosen what appeared to be the most consistent; but if I am to pay any attention to the time named by Admiral Kimberley, the Calliope, in this first stage of her escape, must have taken more than two hours to cover less than four cables. As she thus crept seaward, she buried bow and stem alternately under the billows.

In the fairway of the entrance the flagship Trenton still held on. Her rudder was broken, her wheel carried away; within she was flooded with water from the peccant hawse-pipes; she had just made the signal "fires extinguished," and lay helpless, awaiting the inevitable end. Between this melancholy hulk and the external reef Kane must find a path. Steering within fifty yards of the reef (for which she was actually headed) and her foreyard passing on the other hand over the Trenton's quarter as she rolled, the Calliope sheered between the rival dangers, came to the wind triumphantly, and was once more pointed for the sea and safety. Not often in naval history was there a moment of more sickening peril, and it was dignified by one of those incidents that reconcile the chronicler with his otherwise abhorrent task. From the doomed flagship the Americans hailed the success of the English with a cheer. It was led by the old admiral in person, rang out over the storm with holiday vigour, and was answered by the Calliopes with an emotion easily conceived. This ship of their kinsfolk was almost the last external object seen from the Calliope for hours; immediately after, the mists closed about her till the morrow. She was safe at sea again—una de multis—with a damaged foreyard, and a loss of all the ornamental work about her bow and stern, three anchors, one kedge-anchor, fourteen lengths of chain, four boats, the jib-boom, bobstay, and bands and fastenings of the bowsprit.

Shortly after Kane had slipped his cable, Captain Schoonmaker, despairing of the Vandalia, succeeded in passing astern of the Olga, in the hope to beach his ship beside the Nipsic. At a quarter to eleven her stern took the reef, her hand swung to starboard, and she began to fill and settle. Many lives of brave men were sacrificed in the attempt to get a line ashore; the captain, exhausted by his exertions, was swept from deck by a sea; and the rail being soon awash, the survivors took refuge in the tops.

Out of thirteen that had lain there the day before, there were now but two ships afloat in Apia harbour, and one of these was doomed to be the bane of the other. About 3 P.M. the Trenton parted one cable, and shortly after a second. It was sought to keep her head to wind with storm-sails and by the ingenious expedient of filling the rigging with seamen; but in the fury of the gale, and in that sea, perturbed alike by the gigantic billows and the volleying discharges of the rivers, the rudderless ship drove down stern foremost into the inner basin; ranging, plunging, and striking like a frightened horse; drifting on destruction for herself and bringing it to others. Twice the Olga (still well under command) avoided her impact by the skilful use of helm and engines. But about four the vigilance of the Germans was deceived, and the ships collided; the Olga cutting into the Trenton's quarters, first from one side, then from the other, and losing at the same time two of her own cables. Captain von Ehrhardt instantly slipped the remainder of his moorings, and setting fore and aft canvas, and going full steam ahead, succeeded in beaching his ship in Matautu; whither Knappe, recalled by this new disaster, had returned. The berth was perhaps the best in the harbour, and von Ehrhardt signalled that ship and crew were in security.

The Trenton, guided apparently by an under-tow or eddy from the discharge of the Vaisingano, followed in the course of the Nipsic and Vandalia, and skirted south-eastward along the front of the shore reef, which her keel was at times almost touching. Hitherto she had brought disaster to her foes; now she was bringing it to friends. She had already proved the ruin of the Olga, the one ship that had rid out the hurricane in safety; now she beheld across her course the submerged Vandalia, the tops filled with exhausted seamen.

Happily the approach of the Trenton was gradual, and the time employed to advantage. Rockets and lines were thrown into the tops of the friendly wreck; the approach of danger was transformed into a means of safety; and before the ships struck, the men from the Vandalia's main and mizzen masts, which went immediately by the board in the collision, were already mustered on the Trenton's decks. Those from the foremast were next rescued; and the flagship settled gradually into a position alongside her neighbour, against which she beat all night with violence. Out of the crew of the Vandalia forty-three had perished; of the four hundred and fifty on board the Trenton, only one.

The night of the 16th was still notable for a howling tempest and extraordinary floods of rain. It was feared the wreck could scarce continue to endure the breaching of the seas; among the Germans, the fate of those on board the Adler awoke keen anxiety; and Knappe, on the beach of Matautu, and the other officers of his consulate on that of Matafele, watched all night. The morning of the 17th displayed a scene of devastation rarely equalled: the Adler high and dry, the Olga and Nipsic beached, the Trenton partly piled on the Vandalia and herself sunk to the gun-deck; no sail afloat; and the beach heaped high with the débris of ships and the wreck of mountain forests. Already, before the day, Seumanu, the chief of Apia, had gallantly ventured forth by boat through the subsiding fury of the seas, and had succeeded in communicating with the admiral; already, or as soon after as the dawn permitted, rescue lines were rigged, and the survivors were with difficulty and danger begun to be brought to shore. And soon the cheerful spirit of the admiral added a new feature to the scene. Surrounded as he was by the crews of two wrecked ships, he paraded the band of the Trenton, and the bay was suddenly enlivened with the strains of "Hail Columbia."

During a great part of the day the work of rescue was continued, with many instances of courage and devotion; and for a long time succeeding, the almost inexhaustible harvest of the beach was to be reaped. In the first employment, the Samoans earned the gratitude of friend and foe; in the second, they surprised all by an unexpected virtue, that of honesty. The greatness of the disaster, and the magnitude of the treasure now rolling at their feet, may perhaps have roused in their bosoms an emotion too serious for the rule of greed, or perhaps that greed was for the moment satiated. Sails that twelve strong Samoans could scarce drag from the water, great guns (one of which was rolled by the sea on the body of a man, the only native slain in all the hurricane), an infinite wealth of rope and wood, of tools and weapons, tossed upon the beach. Yet I have never heard that much was stolen; and beyond question, much was very honestly returned. On both accounts, for the saving of life and the restoration of property, the government of the United States showed themselves generous in reward. A fine boat was fitly presented to Seumanu; and rings, watches, and money were lavished on all who had assisted. The Germans also gave money at the rate (as I receive the tale) of three dollars a head for every German saved. The obligation was in this instance incommensurably deep, those with whom they were at war had saved the German blue-jackets at the venture of their lives; Knappe was, besides, far from ungenerous; and I can only explain the niggard figure by supposing it was paid from his own pocket. In one case, at least, it was refused. "I have saved three Germans," said the rescuer; "I will make you a present of the three."

The crews of the American and German squadrons were now cast, still in a bellicose temper, together on the beach. The discipline of the Americans was notoriously loose; the crew of the Nipsic had earned a character for lawlessness in other ports; and recourse was had to stringent and indeed extraordinary measures. The town was divided in two camps, to which the different nationalities were confined. Kimberley had his quarter sentinelled and patrolled. Any seaman disregarding a challenge was to be shot dead; any tavern-keeper who sold spirits to an American sailor was to have his tavern broken and his stock destroyed. Many of the publicans were German; and Knappe, having narrated these rigorous but necessary dispositions, wonders (grinning to himself over his despatch) how far these Americans will go in their assumption of jurisdiction over Germans. Such as they were, the measures were successful. The incongruous mass of castaways was kept in peace, and at last shipped in peace out of the islands.

Kane returned to Apia on the 19th, to find the Calliope the sole survivor of thirteen sail. He thanked his men, and in particular the engineers, in a speech of unusual feeling and beauty, of which one who was present remarked to another, as they left the ship, "This has been a means of grace." Nor did he forget to thank and compliment the admiral; and I cannot deny myself the pleasure of transcribing from Kimberley's reply some generous and engaging words. "My dear captain," he wrote, "your kind note received. You went out splendidly, and we all felt from our hearts for you, and our cheers came with sincerity and admiration for the able manner in which you handled your ship. We could not have been gladder if it had been one of our ships, for in a time like that I can truly say with old Admiral Josiah Latnall, 'that blood is thicker than water.'" One more trait will serve to build up the image of this typical sea-officer. A tiny schooner, the Equator, Captain Edwin Reid, dear to myself from the memories of a six months' cruise, lived out upon the high seas the fury of that tempest which had piled with wrecks the harbour of Apia, found a refuge in Pango-Pango, and arrived at last in the desolated port with a welcome and lucrative cargo of pigs. The admiral was glad to have the pigs; but what most delighted the man's noble and childish soul, was to see once more afloat the colours of his country.

Thus, in what seemed the very article of war, and within the duration of a single day, the sword-arm of each of the two angry Powers was broken; their formidable ships reduced to junk; their disciplined hundreds to a horde of castaways, fed with difficulty, and the fear of whose misconduct marred the sleep of their commanders. Both paused aghast; both had time to recognise that not the whole Samoan Archipelago was worth the loss in men and costly ships already suffered. The so-called hurricane of March 16th made thus a marking epoch in world-history; directly, and at once, it brought about the congress and treaty of Berlin; indirectly, and by a process still continuing, it founded the modern navy of the States. Coming years and other historians will declare the influence of that.

CHAPTER XI—LAUPEPA AND MATAAFA

1889-1892

With the hurricane, the broken war-ships, and the stranded sailors, I am at an end of violence, and my tale flows henceforth among carpet incidents. The blue-jackets on Apia beach were still jealously held apart by sentries, when the powers at home were already seeking a peaceable solution. It was agreed, so far as might be, to obliterate two years of blundering; and to resume in 1889, and at Berlin, those negotiations which had been so unhappily broken off at Washington in 1887. The example thus offered by Germany is rare in history; in the career of Prince Bismarck, so far as I am instructed, it should stand unique. On a review of these two years of blundering, bullying, and failure in a little isle of the Pacific, he seems magnanimously to have owned his policy was in the wrong. He left Fangalii unexpiated; suffered that house of cards, the Tamasese government, to fall by its own frailty and without remark or lamentation; left the Samoan question openly and fairly to the conference: and in the meanwhile, to allay the local heats engendered by Becker and Knappe, he sent to Apia that invaluable public servant, Dr. Stuebel. I should be a dishonest man if I did not bear testimony to the loyalty since shown by Germans in Samoa. Their position was painful; they had talked big in the old days, now they had to sing small. Even Stuebel returned to the islands under the prejudice of an unfortunate record. To the minds of the Samoans his name represented the beginning of their sorrows; and in his first term of office he had unquestionably driven hard. The greater his merit in the surprising success of the second. So long as he stayed, the current of affairs moved smoothly; he left behind him on his departure all men at peace; and whether by fortune, or for the want of that wise hand of guidance, he was scarce gone before the clouds began to gather once more on our horizon.

Before the first convention, Germany and the States hauled down their flags. It was so done again before the second; and Germany, by a still more emphatic step of retrogression, returned the exile Laupepa to his native shores. For two years the unfortunate man had trembled and suffered in the Cameroons, in Germany, in the rainy Marshalls. When he left (September 1887) Tamasese was king, served by five iron war-ships; his right to rule (like a dogma of the Church) was placed outside dispute; the Germans were still, as they were called at that last tearful interview in the house by the river, "the invincible strangers"; the thought of resistance, far less the hope of success, had not yet dawned on the Samoan mind. He returned (November 1889) to a changed world. The Tupua party was reduced to sue for peace, Brandeis was withdrawn, Tamasese was dying obscurely of a broken heart; the German flag no longer waved over the capital; and over all the islands one figure stood supreme. During Laupepa's absence this man had succeeded him in all his honours and titles, in tenfold more than all his power and popularity. He was the idol of the whole nation but the rump of the Tamaseses, and of these he was already the secret admiration. In his position there was but one weak point,—that he had even been tacitly excluded by the Germans. Becker, indeed, once coquetted with the thought of patronising him; but the project had no sequel, and it stands alone. In every other juncture of history the German attitude has been the same. Choose whom you will to be king; when he has failed, choose whom you please to succeed him; when the second fails also, replace the first: upon the one condition, that Mataafa be excluded. "Pourvu qu'il sache signer!"—an official is said to have thus summed up the qualifications necessary in a Samoan king. And it was perhaps feared that Mataafa could do no more and might not always do so much. But this original diffidence was heightened by late events to something verging upon animosity. Fangalii was unavenged: the arms of Mataafa were

Nondum inexpiatis uncta cruoribus,

Still soiled with the unexpiated blood

of German sailors; and though the chief was not present in the field, nor could have heard of the affair till it was over, he had reaped from it credit with his countrymen and dislike from the Germans.

I may not say that trouble was hoped. I must say—if it were not feared, the practice of diplomacy must teach a very hopeful view of human nature. Mataafa and Laupepa, by the sudden repatriation of the last, found themselves face to face in conditions of exasperating rivalry. The one returned from the dead of exile to find himself replaced and excelled. The other, at the end of a long, anxious, and successful struggle, beheld his only possible competitor resuscitated from the grave. The qualities of both, in this difficult moment, shone out nobly. I feel I seem always less than partial to the lovable Laupepa; his virtues are perhaps not those which chiefly please me, and are certainly not royal; but he found on his return an opportunity to display the admirable sweetness of his nature. The two entered into a competition of generosity, for which I can recall no parallel in history, each waiving the throne for himself, each pressing it upon his rival; and they embraced at last a compromise the terms of which seem to have been always obscure and are now disputed. Laupepa at least resumed his style of King of Samoa; Mataafa retained much of the conduct of affairs, and continued to receive much of the attendance and respect befitting royalty; and the two Malietoas, with so many causes of disunion, dwelt and met together in the same town like kinsmen. It was so, that I first saw them; so, in a house set about with sentries—for there was still a haunting fear of Germany,—that I heard them relate their various experience in the past; heard Laupepa tell with touching candour of the sorrows of his exile, and Mataafa with mirthful simplicity of his resources and anxieties in the war. The relation was perhaps too beautiful to last; it was perhaps impossible but the titular king should grow at last uneasily conscious of the maire de palais at his side, or the king-maker be at last offended by some shadow of distrust or assumption in his creature. I repeat the words king-maker and creature; it is so that Mataafa himself conceives of their relation: surely not without justice; for, had he not contended and prevailed, and been helped by the folly of consuls and the fury of the storm, Laupepa must have died in exile.

Foreigners in these islands know little of the course of native intrigue. Partly the Samoans cannot explain, partly they will not tell. Ask how much a master can follow of the puerile politics in any school; so much and no more we may understand of the events which surround and menace us with their results. The missions may perhaps have been to blame. Missionaries are perhaps apt to meddle overmuch outside their discipline; it is a fault which should be judged with mercy; the problem is sometimes so insidiously presented that even a moderate and able man is betrayed beyond his own intention; and the missionary in such a land as Samoa is something else besides a minister of mere religion; he represents civilisation, he is condemned to be an organ of reform, he could scarce evade (even if he desired) a certain influence in political affairs. And it is believed, besides, by those who fancy they know, that the effective force of division between Mataafa and Laupepa came from the natives rather than from whites. Before the end of 1890, at least, it began to be rumoured that there was dispeace between the two Malietoas; and doubtless this had an unsettling influence throughout the islands. But there was another ingredient of anxiety. The Berlin convention had long closed its sittings; the text of the Act had been long in our hands; commissioners were announced to right the wrongs of the land question, and two high officials, a chief justice and a president, to guide policy and administer law in Samoa. Their coming was expected with an impatience, with a childishness of trust, that can hardly be exaggerated. Months passed, these angel-deliverers still delayed to arrive, and the impatience of the natives became changed to an ominous irritation. They have had much experience of being deceived, and they began to think they were deceived again. A sudden crop of superstitious stories buzzed about the islands. Rivers had come down red; unknown fishes had been taken on the reef and found to be marked with menacing runes; a headless lizard crawled among chiefs in council; the gods of Upolu and Savaii made war by night, they swam the straits to battle, and, defaced by dreadful wounds, they had besieged the house of a medical missionary. Readers will remember the portents in mediæval chronicles, or those in Julius Cæsar when

> "Fierce fiery warriors fought upon the clouds
>
> In ranks and squadrons."

And doubtless such fabrications are, in simple societies, a natural expression of discontent; and those who forge, and even those who spread them, work towards a conscious purpose.

Early in January 1891 this period of expectancy was brought to an end by the arrival of Conrad Cedarcrantz, chief justice of Samoa. The event was hailed with acclamation, and there was much about the new official to increase the hopes already entertained. He was seen to be a man of culture and ability; in public, of an excellent presence—in private, of a most engaging cordiality. But there was one point, I scarce know whether to say of his character or policy, which immediately and disastrously affected public feeling in the islands. He had an aversion, part judicial, part perhaps constitutional, to haste; and he announced that, until he should have well satisfied his own mind, he should do nothing; that he would rather delay all than do aught amiss. It was impossible to hear this without academical approval; impossible to hear it without practical alarm. The natives desired to see activity; they desired to see many fair speeches taken on a body of deeds and works of benefit. Fired by the event of the war, filled with impossible hopes, they might have welcomed in that hour a ruler of the stamp of Brandeis, breathing hurry, perhaps dealing blows. And the chief justice, unconscious of the fleeting opportunity, ripened his opinions deliberately in Mulinuu; and had been already the better part of half a year in the islands before he went through the form of opening his court. The curtain had risen; there was no play. A reaction, a chill sense of disappointment, passed about the island; and intrigue, one moment suspended, was resumed.

In the Berlin Act, the three Powers recognise, on the threshold, "the independence of the Samoan government, and the free right of the natives to elect their chief or king and choose their form of government." True, the text continues that, "in view of the difficulties that surround an election in the present disordered condition of the government," Malietoa Laupepa shall be recognised as king, "unless the three Powers shall by common accord otherwise declare." But perhaps few natives have followed it so far, and even those who have, were possibly all cast abroad again by the next clause: "and his successor shall be duly elected according to the laws and customs of Samoa." The right to elect, freely given in one sentence, was suspended in the next, and a line or so further on appeared to be reconveyed by a side-wind. The reason offered for suspension was ludicrously false; in May 1889, when Sir Edward Malet moved the matter in the conference, the election of Mataafa was not only certain to have been peaceful, it could not have been opposed;

and behind the English puppet it was easy to suspect the hand of Germany. No one is more swift to smell trickery than a Samoan; and the thought, that, under the long, bland, benevolent sentences of the Berlin Act, some trickery lay lurking, filled him with the breath of opposition. Laupepa seems never to have been a popular king. Mataafa, on the other hand, holds an unrivalled position in the eyes of his fellow-countrymen; he was the hero of the war, he had lain with them in the bush, he had borne the heat and burthen of the day; they began to claim that he should enjoy more largely the fruits of victory; his exclusion was believed to be a stroke of German vengeance, his elevation to the kingship was looked for as the fitting crown and copestone of the Samoan triumph; and but a little after the coming of the chief justice, an ominous cry for Mataafa began to arise in the islands. It is difficult to see what that official could have done but what he did. He was loyal, as in duty bound, to the treaty and to Laupepa; and when the orators of the important and unruly islet of Manono demanded to his face a change of kings, he had no choice but to refuse them, and (his reproof being unheeded) to suspend the meeting. Whether by any neglect of his own or the mere force of circumstance, he failed, however, to secure the sympathy, failed even to gain the confidence, of Mataafa. The latter is not without a sense of his own abilities or of the great service he has rendered to his native land. He felt himself neglected; at the very moment when the cry for his elevation rang throughout the group he thought himself made little of on Mulinuu; and he began to weary of his part. In this humour, he was exposed to a temptation which I must try to explain, as best I may be able, to Europeans.

The bestowal of the great name, Malietoa, is in the power of the district of Malie, some seven miles to the westward of Apia. The most noisy and conspicuous supporters of that party are the inhabitants of Manono. Hence in the elaborate, allusive oratory of Samoa, Malie is always referred to by the name of Pule (authority) as having the power of the name, and Manono by that of Ainga (clan, sept, or household) as forming the immediate family of the chief. But these, though so important, are only small communities; and perhaps the chief numerical force of the Malietoas inhabits the island of Savaii. Savaii has no royal name to bestow, all the five being in the gift of different districts of Upolu; but she has the weight of numbers, and in these latter days has acquired a certain force by the preponderance in her councils of a single man, the orator Lauati. The reader will now understand the peculiar significance of a deputation which should embrace Lauati and the orators of both Malie and Manono, how it would represent all that is most effective on the Malietoa side, and all that is most considerable in Samoan politics, except the opposite feudal party of the Tupua. And in the temptation brought to bear on Mataafa, even the Tupua was conjoined. Tamasese was dead. His followers had conceived a not unnatural aversion to all Germans, from which only the loyal Brandeis is excepted; and a not unnatural admiration for their late successful adversary. Men of his own blood and clan, men whom he had fought in the field, whom he had driven from Matautu, who had smitten him back time and again from before the rustic bulwarks of Lotoanuu, they approached him hand in hand with their ancestral enemies and concurred in the same prayer. The treaty (they argued) was not carried out. The right to elect their king had been granted them; or if that were denied or suspended, then the right to elect "his successor." They were dissatisfied with Laupepa, and claimed, "according to the laws and customs of Samoa," duly to appoint another. The orators of Malie declared with irritation that their second appointment was alone valid and Mataafa the sole Malietoa; the whole body of malcontents named him as their choice for king; and they requested him in consequence to leave Apia and take up his dwelling in Malie, the name-place of Malietoa; a step which may be described, to European ears, as placing before the country his candidacy for the crown.

I do not know when the proposal was first made. Doubtless the disaffection grew slowly, every trifle adding to its force; doubtless there lingered for long a willingness to give the new government a trial. The chief justice at least had been nearly five months in the country, and the president, Baron Senfft von Pilsach, rather more than a month before the mine was sprung. On May 31, 1891, the house of Mataafa was found empty, he and his chiefs had vanished from Apia, and, what was worse, three prisoners, liberated from the gaol, had accompanied them in their secession; two being political offenders, and the third (accused of murder) having been perhaps set free by accident. Although the step had been discussed in certain quarters, it took all men by surprise. The inhabitants at large expected instant war. The

140

officials awakened from a dream to recognise the value of that which they had lost. Mataafa at Vaiala, where he was the pledge of peace, had perhaps not always been deemed worthy of particular attention; Mataafa at Malie was seen, twelve hours too late, to be an altogether different quantity. With excess of zeal on the other side, the officials trooped to their boats and proceeded almost in a body to Malie, where they seem to have employed every artifice of flattery and every resource of eloquence upon the fugitive high chief. These courtesies, perhaps excessive in themselves, had the unpardonable fault of being offered when too late. Mataafa showed himself facile on small issues, inflexible on the main; he restored the prisoners, he returned with the consuls to Apia on a flying visit; he gave his word that peace should be preserved—a pledge in which perhaps no one believed at the moment, but which he has since nobly redeemed. On the rest he was immovable; he had cast the die, he had declared his candidacy, he had gone to Malie. Thither, after his visit to Apia, he returned again; there he has practically since resided.

Thus was created in the islands a situation, strange in the beginning, and which, as its inner significance is developed, becomes daily stranger to observe. On the one hand, Mataafa sits in Malie, assumes a regal state, receives deputations, heads his letters "Government of Samoa," tacitly treats the king as a co-ordinate; and yet declares himself, and in many ways conducts himself, as a law-abiding citizen. On the other, the white officials in Mulinuu stand contemplating the phenomenon with eyes of growing stupefaction; now with symptoms of collapse, now with accesses of violence. For long, even those well versed in island manners and the island character daily expected war, and heard imaginary drums beat in the forest. But for now close upon a year, and against every stress of persuasion and temptation, Mataafa has been the bulwark of our peace. Apia lay open to be seized, he had the power in his hand, his followers cried to be led on, his enemies marshalled him the same way by impotent examples; and he has never faltered. Early in the day, a white man was sent from the government of Mulinuu to examine and report upon his actions: I saw the spy on his return; "It was only our rebel that saved us," he said, with a laugh. There is now no honest man in the islands but is well aware of it; none but knows that, if we have enjoyed during the past eleven months the conveniences of peace, it is due to the forbearance of "our rebel." Nor does this part of his conduct stand alone. He calls his party at Malie the government,—"our government,"—but he pays his taxes to the government at Mulinuu. He takes ground like a king; he has steadily and blandly refused to obey all orders as to his own movements or behaviour; but upon requisition he sends offenders to be tried under the chief justice.

We have here a problem of conduct, and what seems an image of inconsistency, very hard at the first sight to be solved by any European. Plainly Mataafa does not act at random. Plainly, in the depths of his Samoan mind, he regards his attitude as regular and constitutional. It may be unexpected, it may be inauspicious, it may be undesirable; but he thinks it—and perhaps it is—in full accordance with those "laws and customs of Samoa" ignorantly invoked by the draughtsmen of the Berlin Act. The point is worth an effort of comprehension; a man's life may yet depend upon it. Let us conceive, in the first place, that there are five separate kingships in Samoa, though not always five different kings; and that though one man, by holding the five royal names, might become king in all parts of Samoa, there is perhaps no such matter as a kingship of all Samoa. He who holds one royal name would be, upon this view, as much a sovereign person as he who should chance to hold the other four; he would have less territory and fewer subjects, but the like independence and an equal royalty. Now Mataafa, even if all debatable points were decided against him, is still Tuiatua, and as such, on this hypothesis, a sovereign prince. In the second place, the draughtsmen of the Act, waxing exceeding bold, employed the word "election," and implicitly justified all precedented steps towards the kingship according with the "customs of Samoa." I am not asking what was intended by the gentlemen who sat and debated very benignly and, on the whole, wisely in Berlin; I am asking what will be understood by a Samoan studying their literary work, the Berlin Act; I am asking what is the result of taking a word out of one state of society, and applying it to another, of which the writers know less than nothing, and no European knows much. Several interpreters and several days were employed last September in the fruitless attempt to convey to the mind of Laupepa the sense of the word "resignation." What can a Samoan gather from the words, election? election of a king? election of a king according to the laws and customs of Samoa? What are the electoral measures, what is the method of canvassing, likely to be employed by two, three, four, or five, more or less absolute princelings, eager to evince each other? And who is to distinguish such a process from the state of war? In such international—or, I should say, interparochial—differences, the nearest we can come towards understanding is to appreciate the cloud of ambiguity in which all parties grope—

"Treading the crude consistence, half on foot,

Half flying."

Now, in one part of Mataafa's behaviour his purpose is beyond mistake. Towards the provisions of the Berlin Act, his desire to be formally obedient is manifest. The Act imposed the tax. He has paid his taxes, although he thus contributes to the ways and means of his immediate rival. The Act decreed the supreme court, and he sends his partisans to be tried at Mulinuu, although he thus places them (as I shall have occasion to show) in a position far from wholly safe. From this literal conformity, in matters regulated, to the terms of the Berlin plenipotentiaries, we may plausibly infer, in regard to the rest, a no less exact observance of the famous and obscure "laws and customs of Samoa."

But though it may be possible to attain, in the study, to some such adumbration of an understanding, it were plainly unfair to expect it of officials in the hurry of events. Our two white officers have accordingly been no more perspicacious than was to be looked for, and I think they have sometimes been less wise. It was not wise in the president to proclaim Mataafa and his followers rebels and their estates confiscated. Such words are not respectable till they repose on force; on the lips of an angry white man, standing alone on a small promontory, they were both dangerous and absurd; they might have provoked ruin; thanks to the character of Mataafa, they only raised a smile and damaged the authority of government. And again it is not wise in the government of Mulinuu to have twice attempted to precipitate hostilities, once in Savaii, once here in the Tuamasanga. The fate of the Savaii attempt I never heard; it seems to have been stillborn. The other passed under my eyes. A war-party was armed in Apia, and despatched across the island

143

against Mataafa villages, where it was to seize the women and children. It was absent for some days, engaged in feasting with those whom it went out to fight; and returned at last, innocuous and replete. In this fortunate though undignified ending we may read the fact that the natives on Laupepa's side are sometimes more wise than their advisers. Indeed, for our last twelve months of miraculous peace under what seem to be two rival kings, the credit is due first of all to Mataafa, and second to the half-heartedness, or the forbearance, or both, of the natives in the other camp. The voice of the two whites has ever been for war. They have published at least one incendiary proclamation; they have armed and sent into the field at least one Samoan war-party; they have continually besieged captains of war-ships to attack Malie, and the captains of the war-ships have religiously refused. Thus in the last twelve months our European rulers have drawn a picture of themselves, as bearded like the pard, full of strange oaths, and gesticulating like semaphores; while over against them Mataafa reposes smilingly obstinate, and their own retainers surround them, frowningly inert. Into the question of motive I refuse to enter; but if we come to war in these islands, and with no fresh occasion, it will be a manufactured war, and one that has been manufactured, against the grain of opinion, by two foreigners.

For the last and worst of the mistakes on the Laupepa side it would be unfair to blame any but the king himself. Capable both of virtuous resolutions and of fits of apathetic obstinacy, His Majesty is usually the whip-top of competitive advisers; and his conduct is so unstable as to wear at times an appearance of treachery which would surprise himself if he could see it. Take, for example, the experience of Lieutenant Ulfsparre, late chief of police, and (so to speak) commander of the forces. His men were under orders for a certain hour; he found himself almost alone at the place of muster, and learned the king had sent the soldiery on errands. He sought an audience, explained that he was here to implant discipline, that (with this purpose in view) his men could only receive orders through himself, and if that condition were not agreed to and faithfully observed, he must send in his papers. The king was as usual easily persuaded, the interview passed and ended to the satisfaction of all parties engaged—and the bargain was kept for one day. On the day after, the troops were again dispersed as post-runners, and their commander resigned. With such a sovereign, I repeat, it would be unfair to blame any individual minister for any specific fault. And yet the policy of our two whites against Mataafa has appeared uniformly so excessive and implacable, that the blame of the last scandal is laid generally at their doors. It is yet fresh. Lauati, towards the end of last year, became deeply concerned about the situation; and by great personal exertions and the charms of oratory brought Savaii and Manono into agreement upon certain terms of compromise: Laupepa still to be king, Mataafa to accept a high executive office comparable to that of our own prime minister, and the two governments to coalesce. Intractable Manono was a party. Malie was said to view the proposal with resignation, if not relief. Peace was thought secure. The night before the king was to receive Lauati, I met one of his company,—the family chief, Iina,—and we shook hands over the unexpected issue of our troubles. What no one dreamed was that Laupepa would refuse. And he did. He refused undisputed royalty for himself and peace for these unhappy islands; and the two whites on Mulinuu rightly or wrongly got the blame of it.

But their policy has another and a more awkward side. About the time of the secession to Malie, many ugly things were said; I will not repeat that which I hope and believe the speakers did not wholly mean; let it suffice that, if rumour carried to Mataafa the language I have heard used in my own house and before my own native servants, he would be highly justified in keeping clear of Apia and the whites. One gentleman whose opinion I respect, and am so bold as to hope I may in some points modify, will understand the allusion and appreciate my reserve. About the same time there occurred an incident, upon which I must be more particular. A was a gentleman who had long been an intimate of Mataafa's, and had recently (upon account, indeed, of the secession to Malie) more or less wholly broken off relations. To him came one whom I shall call B with a dastardly proposition. It may have been B's own, in which case he were the more unpardonable; but from the closeness of his intercourse with the chief justice, as well as from the terms used in the interview, men judged otherwise. It was proposed that A should simulate a renewal of the friendship, decoy Mataafa to a suitable place, and have him there arrested. What should follow in those days of violent speech was at the least disputable; and the proposal was of course refused. "You do

145

not understand," was the base rejoinder. "You will have no discredit. The Germans are to take the blame of the arrest." Of course, upon the testimony of a gentleman so depraved, it were unfair to hang a dog; and both the Germans and the chief justice must be held innocent. But the chief justice has shown that he can himself be led, by his animosity against Mataafa, into questionable acts. Certain natives of Malie were accused of stealing pigs; the chief justice summoned them through Mataafa; several were sent, and along with them a written promise that, if others were required, these also should be forthcoming upon requisition. Such as came were duly tried and acquitted; and Mataafa's offer was communicated to the chief justice, who made a formal answer, and the same day (in pursuance of his constant design to have Malie attacked by war-ships) reported to one of the consuls that his warrant would not run in the country and that certain of the accused had been withheld. At least, this is not fair dealing; and the next instance I have to give is possibly worse. For one blunder the chief justice is only so far responsible, in that he was not present where it seems he should have been, when it was made. He had nothing to do with the silly proscription of the Mataafas; he has always disliked the measure; and it occurred to him at last that he might get rid of this dangerous absurdity and at the same time reap a further advantage. Let Mataafa leave Malie for any other district in Samoa; it should be construed as an act of submission and the confiscation and proscription instantly recalled. This was certainly well devised; the government escaped from their own false position, and by the same stroke lowered the prestige of their adversaries. But unhappily the chief justice did not put all his eggs in one basket. Concurrently with these negotiations he began again to move the captain of one of the war-ships to shell the rebel village; the captain, conceiving the extremity wholly unjustified, not only refused these instances, but more or less publicly complained of their being made; the matter came to the knowledge of the white resident who was at that time playing the part of intermediary with Malie; and he, in natural anger and disgust, withdrew from the negotiation. These duplicities, always deplorable when discovered, are never more fatal than with men imperfectly civilised. Almost incapable of truth themselves, they cherish a particular score of the same fault in whites. And Mataafa is besides an exceptional native. I would scarce dare say of any Samoan that he is truthful, though I seem to have encountered the phenomenon; but I must say of Mataafa that he seems distinctly and consistently averse to lying.

For the affair of the Manono prisoners, the chief justice is only again in so far answerable as he was at the moment absent from the seat of his duties; and the blame falls on Baron Senfft von Pilsach, president of the municipal council. There were in Manono certain dissidents, loyal to Laupepa. Being Manono people, I daresay they were very annoying to their neighbours; the majority, as they belonged to the same island, were the more impatient; and one fine day fell upon and destroyed the houses and harvests of the dissidents "according to the laws and customs of Samoa." The president went down to the unruly island in a war-ship and was landed alone upon the beach. To one so much a stranger to the mansuetude of Polynesians, this must have seemed an act of desperation; and the baron's gallantry met with a deserved success. The six ringleaders, acting in Mataafa's interest, had been guilty of a delict; with Mataafa's approval, they delivered themselves over to be tried. On Friday, September 4, 1891, they were convicted before a native magistrate and sentenced to six months' imprisonment; or, I should rather say, detention; for it was expressly directed that they were to be used as gentlemen and not as prisoners, that the door was to stand open, and that all their wishes should be gratified. This extraordinary sentence fell upon the accused like a thunderbolt. There is no need to suppose perfidy, where a careless interpreter suffices to explain all; but the six chiefs claim to have understood their coming to Apia as an act of submission merely formal, that they came in fact under an implied indemnity, and that the president stood pledged to see them scatheless. Already, on their way from the court-house, they were tumultuously surrounded by friends and clansmen, who pressed and cried upon them to escape; Lieutenant Ulfsparre must order his men to load; and with that the momentary effervescence died away. Next day, Saturday, 5th, the chief justice took his departure from the islands—a step never yet explained and (in view of the doings of the day before and the remonstrances of other officials) hard to justify. The president, an amiable and brave young man of singular inexperience, was thus left to face the growing difficulty by himself. The clansmen of the prisoners, to the number of near upon a hundred, lay in Vaiusu, a village half way between Apia and Malie; there they talked big, thence sent menacing messages; the gaol should be broken in the night, they said, and the six martyrs rescued. Allowance is to be made for the character of the people of Manono, turbulent fellows, boastful of tongue, but of late days not thought to be answerably bold in person. Yet the moment was anxious. The government of Mulinuu had gained an important moral victory by the surrender and condemnation of the chiefs; and it was needful the victory should be maintained. The guard upon the gaol was accordingly strengthened; a war-party was sent to watch the Vaiusu road under Asi; and the chiefs of the Vaimaunga were notified to arm and assemble their men. It must be supposed the president was doubtful of the loyalty of these assistants. He turned at least to the war-ships, where it seems he was rebuffed; thence he fled into the arms of the wrecker gang, where he was unhappily more successful. The government of Washington had presented to the Samoan king the wrecks of the Trenton and the Vandalia; an American syndicate had been formed to break them up; an experienced gang was in consequence settled in Apia and the report of submarine explosions had long grown familiar in the ears of residents. From these artificers the president obtained a supply of dynamite, the needful mechanism, and the loan of a mechanic; the gaol was mined, and the Manono people in Vaiusu were advertised of the fact in a letter signed by Laupepa. Partly by the indiscretion of the mechanic, who had sought to embolden himself (like Lady Macbeth) with liquor for his somewhat dreadful task, the story leaked immediately out and raised a very general, or I might say almost universal, reprobation. Some blamed the proposed deed because it was barbarous and a foul example to set before a race half barbarous itself; others because it was illegal; others again because, in the face of so weak an enemy, it appeared pitifully pusillanimous; almost all because it tended to precipitate and embitter war. In the midst of the turmoil he had raised, and under the immediate pressure of certain indignant white residents, the baron fell back upon a new expedient, certainly less barbarous, perhaps no more legal; and on Monday afternoon, September 7th, packed his six prisoners on board the cutter Lancashire Lass, and deported them to the neighbouring low-island group of the Tokelaus. We watched her put to sea with mingled feelings. Anything were better than dynamite, but this was not good. The men had been summoned in the name of law; they had surrendered; the law had uttered its voice; they were under one sentence duly delivered; and now the president, by no right with which we were acquainted, had exchanged it for another. It was perhaps no less fortunate, though it was more pardonable in a stranger, that he had increased the punishment to that which, in the eyes of Samoans, ranks next to death,—exile from their native land and friends. And the Lancashire Lass appeared to carry away with her into the uttermost parts of the sea the honour of the administration and the prestige of the supreme court.

The policy of the government towards Mataafa has thus been of a piece throughout; always would-be violent, it has been almost always defaced with some appearance of perfidy or unfairness. The policy of Mataafa (though extremely bewildering to any white) appears everywhere consistent with itself, and the man's bearing has always been calm. But to represent the fulness of the contrast, it is necessary that I should give some description of the two capitals, or the two camps, and the ways and means of the regular and irregular government.

Mulinuu. Mulinuu, the reader may remember, is a narrow finger of land planted in cocoa-palms, which runs forth into the lagoon perhaps three quarters of a mile. To the east is the bay of Apia. To the west, there is, first of all, a mangrove swamp, the mangroves excellently green, the mud ink-black, and its face crawled upon by countless insects and black and scarlet crabs. Beyond the swamp is a wide and shallow bay of the lagoon, bounded to the west by Faleula Point. Faleula is the next village to Malie; so that from the top of some tall palm in Malie it should be possible to descry against the eastern heavens the palms of Mulinuu. The trade wind sweeps over the low peninsula and cleanses it from the contagion of the swamp. Samoans have a quaint phrase in their language; when out of health, they seek exposed places on the shore "to eat the wind," say they; and there can be few better places for such a diet than the point of Mulinuu.

Two European houses stand conspicuous on the harbour side; in Europe they would seem poor enough, but they are fine houses for Samoa. One is new; it was built the other day under the apologetic title of a Government House, to be the residence of Baron Senfft. The other is historical; it was

built by Brandeis on a mortgage, and is now occupied by the chief justice
on conditions never understood, the rumour going uncontradicted that he
sits rent free. I do not say it is true, I say it goes uncontradicted; and there is
one peculiarity of our officials in a nutshell,—their remarkable indifference
to their own character. From the one house to the other extends a scattering
village for the Faipule or native parliament men. In the days of Tamasese this
was a brave place, both his own house and those of the Faipule good, and the
whole excellently ordered and approached by a sanded way. It is now like a
neglected bush-town, and speaks of apathy in all concerned. But the chief
scandal of Mulinuu is elsewhere. The house of the president stands just to
seaward of the isthmus, where the watch is set nightly, and armed men guard
the uneasy slumbers of the government. On the landward side there stands a
monument to the poor German lads who fell at Fangalii, just beyond which
the passer-by may chance to observe a little house standing back-ward from
the road. It is such a house as a commoner might use in a bush village; none
could dream that it gave shelter even to a family chief; yet this is the palace
of Malietoa-Natoaitele-Tamasoalii Laupepa, king of Samoa. As you sit in
his company under this humble shelter, you shall see, between the posts, the
new house of the president. His Majesty himself beholds it daily, and the
tenor of his thoughts may be divined. The fine house of a Samoan chief is
his appropriate attribute; yet, after seventeen months, the government (well
housed themselves) have not yet found—have not yet sought—a roof-tree for
their sovereign. And the lodging is typical. I take up the president's financial
statement of September 8, 1891. I find the king's allowance to figure at
seventy-five dollars a month; and I find that he is further (though somewhat
obscurely) debited with the salaries of either two or three clerks. Take the
outside figure, and the sum expended on or for His Majesty amounts to
ninety-five dollars in the month. Lieutenant Ulfsparre and Dr. Hagberg (the
chief justice's Swedish friends) drew in the same period one hundred and
forty and one hundred dollars respectively on account of salary alone. And
it should be observed that Dr. Hagberg was employed, or at least paid, from
government funds, in the face of His Majesty's express and reiterated protest.
In another column of the statement, one hundred and seventy-five dollars
and seventy-five cents are debited for the chief justice's travelling expenses. I

am of the opinion that if His Majesty desired (or dared) to take an outing, he would be asked to bear the charge from his allowance. But although I think the chief justice had done more nobly to pay for himself, I am far from denying that his excursions were well meant; he should indeed be praised for having made them; and I leave the charge out of consideration in the following statement.

ON THE ONE HAND

Salary of Chief Justice Cedarkrantz $500

Salary of President Baron Senfft von Pilsach (about) 415

Salary of Lieutenant Ulfsparre, Chief of Police 140

Salary of Dr. Hagberg, Private Secretary to the Chief Justice 100

Total monthly salary to four whites, one of them paid against His Majesty's protest $1155

ON THE OTHER HAND

Total monthly payments to and for His Majesty the King, including allowance and hire of three clerks, one of these placed under the rubric of extraordinary expenses $95

This looks strange enough and mean enough already. But we have ground of comparison in the practice of Brandeis.

Brandeis, white prime minister $200

Tamasese (about) 160

White Chief of Police 100

Under Brandeis, in other words, the king received the second highest allowance on the sheet; and it was a good second, and the third was a bad third. And it must be borne in mind that Tamasese himself was pointed and laughed at among natives. Judge, then, what is muttered of Laupepa, housed in his shanty before the president's doors like Lazarus before the doors of Dives; receiving not so much of his own taxes as the private secretary of the law officer; and (in actual salary) little more than half as much as his own chief of police. It is known besides that he has protested in vain against the charge for Dr. Hagberg; it is known that he has himself applied for an advance and been refused. Money is certainly a grave subject on Mulinuu; but respect costs nothing, and thrifty officials might have judged it wise to make up in extra politeness for what they curtailed of pomp or comfort. One instance may suffice. Laupepa appeared last summer on a public occasion; the president was there and not even the president rose to greet the entrance of the sovereign. Since about the same period, besides, the monarch must be described as in a state of sequestration. A white man, an Irishman, the true type of all that is most gallant, humorous, and reckless in his country, chose to visit His Majesty and give him some excellent advice (to make up his difference with Mataafa) couched unhappily in vivid and figurative language. The adviser now sleeps in the Pacific, but the evil that he chanced to do lives after him. His Majesty was greatly (and I must say justly) offended by the freedom of the expressions used; he appealed to his white advisers; and these, whether from want of thought or by design, issued an ignominious proclamation. Intending visitors to the palace must appear before their consuls and justify their business. The majesty of buried Samoa was henceforth only to be viewed (like a private collection) under special permit; and was thus at once cut off from the company and opinions of the self respecting. To retain any dignity in such an abject state would require a man of very different virtues from those claimed by the not unvirtuous Laupepa. He is not designed to ride the whirlwind or direct the storm, rather to be the ornament of private life. He is kind, gentle, patient as Job, conspicuously well-intentioned, of charming manners; and when he pleases, he has one accomplishment in which he now begins to be alone—I mean that he can pronounce correctly his own beautiful language.

The government of Brandeis accomplished a good deal and was continually and heroically attempting more. The government of our two whites has confined itself almost wholly to paying and receiving salaries. They have built, indeed, a house for the president; they are believed (if that be a merit) to have bought the local newspaper with government funds; and their rule has been enlivened by a number of scandals, into which I feel with relief that it is unnecessary I should enter. Even if the three Powers do not remove these gentlemen, their absurd and disastrous government must perish by itself of inanition. Native taxes (except perhaps from Mataafa, true to his own private policy) have long been beyond hope. And only the other day (May 6th, 1892), on the expressed ground that there was no guarantee as to how the funds would be expended, and that the president consistently refused to allow the verification of his cash balances, the municipal council has negatived the proposal to call up further taxes from the whites. All is well that ends even ill, so that it end; and we believe that with the last dollar we shall see the last of the last functionary. Now when it is so nearly over, we can afford to smile at this extraordinary passage, though we must still sigh over the occasion lost.

* * * * *

Malie. The way to Malie lies round the shores of Faleula bay and through a succession of pleasant groves and villages. The road, one of the works of Brandeis, is now cut up by pig fences. Eight times you must leap a barrier of cocoa posts; the take-off and the landing both in a patch of mire planted with big stones, and the stones sometimes reddened with the blood of horses that have gone before. To make these obstacles more annoying, you have sometimes to wait while a black boar clambers sedately over the so-called pig fence. Nothing can more thoroughly depict the worst side of the Samoan character than these useless barriers which deface their only road. It was one of the first orders issued by the government of Mulinuu after the coming of the chief justice, to have the passage cleared. It is the disgrace of Mataafa that the thing is not yet done.

The village of Malie is the scene of prosperity and peace. In a very good account of a visit there, published in the Australasian, the writer describes it to be fortified; she must have been deceived by the appearance of some pig walls on the shore. There is no fortification, no parade of war. I understand that from one to five hundred fighting men are always within reach; but I have never seen more than five together under arms, and these were the king's guard of honour. A Sabbath quiet broods over the well-weeded green, the picketed horses, the troops of pigs, the round or oval native dwellings. Of

153

these there are a surprising number, very fine of their sort: yet more are in the building; and in the midst a tall house of assembly, by far the greatest Samoan structure now in these islands, stands about half finished and already makes a figure in the landscape. No bustle is to be observed, but the work accomplished testifies to a still activity.

The centre-piece of all is the high chief himself, Malietoa-Tuiatua-Tuiaana Mataafa, king—or not king—or king-claimant—of Samoa. All goes to him, all comes from him. Native deputations bring him gifts and are feasted in return. White travellers, to their indescribable irritation, are (on his approach) waved from his path by his armed guards. He summons his dancers by the note of a bugle. He sits nightly at home before a semicircle of talking-men from many quarters of the islands, delivering and hearing those ornate and elegant orations in which the Samoan heart delights. About himself and all his surroundings there breathes a striking sense of order, tranquillity, and native plenty. He is of a tall and powerful person, sixty years of age, white-haired and with a white moustache; his eyes bright and quiet; his jaw perceptibly underhung, which gives him something of the expression of a benevolent mastiff; his manners dignified and a thought insinuating, with an air of a Catholic prelate. He was never married, and a natural daughter attends upon his guests. Long since he made a vow of chastity,—"to live as our Lord lived on this earth" and Polynesians report with bated breath that he has kept it. On all such points, true to his Catholic training, he is inclined to be even rigid. Lauati, the pivot of Savaii, has recently repudiated his wife and taken a fairer; and when I was last in Malie, Mataafa (with a strange superiority to his own interests) had but just despatched a reprimand. In his immediate circle, in spite of the smoothness of his ways, he is said to be more respected than beloved; and his influence is the child rather of authority than popularity. No Samoan grandee now living need have attempted that which he has accomplished during the last twelve months with unimpaired prestige, not only to withhold his followers from war, but to send them to be judged in the camp of their enemies on Mulinuu. And it is a matter of debate whether such a triumph of authority were ever possible before. Speaking for myself, I have visited and dwelt in almost every seat of the Polynesian race, and have met but one man who gave me a stronger impression of character and parts.

About the situation, Mataafa expresses himself with unshaken peace. To the chief justice he refers with some bitterness; to Laupepa, with a smile, as "my poor brother." For himself, he stands upon the treaty, and expects sooner or later an election in which he shall be raised to the chief power. In the meanwhile, or for an alternative, he would willingly embrace a compromise with Laupepa; to which he would probably add one condition, that the joint government should remain seated at Malie, a sensible but not inconvenient distance from white intrigues and white officials. One circumstance in my last interview particularly pleased me. The king's chief scribe, Esela, is an old employé under Tamasese, and the talk ran some while upon the character of Brandeis. Loyalty in this world is after all not thrown away; Brandeis was guilty, in Samoan eyes, of many irritating errors, but he stood true to Tamasese; in the course of time a sense of this virtue and of his general uprightness has obliterated the memory of his mistakes; and it would have done his heart good if he could have heard his old scribe and his old adversary join in praising him. "Yes," concluded Mataafa, "I wish we had Planteisa back again." A quelque chose malheur est bon. So strong is the impression produced by the defects of Cedarcrantz and Baron Senfft, that I believe Mataafa far from singular in this opinion, and that the return of the upright Brandeis might be even welcome to many.

I must add a last touch to the picture of Malie and the pretender's life. About four in the morning, the visitor in his house will be awakened by the note of a pipe, blown without, very softly and to a soothing melody. This is Mataafa's private luxury to lead on pleasant dreams. We have a bird here in Samoa that about the same hour of darkness sings in the bush. The father of Mataafa, while he lived, was a great friend and protector to all living creatures, and passed under the by-name of the King of Birds. It may be it was among the woodland clients of the sire that the son acquired his fancy for this morning music.

* * * * *

I have now sought to render without extenuation the impressions received: of dignity, plenty, and peace at Malie, of bankruptcy and distraction at Mulinuu. And I wish I might here bring to an end ungrateful labours. But

I am sensible that there remain two points on which it would be improper to be silent. I should be blamed if I did not indicate a practical conclusion; and I should blame myself if I did not do a little justice to that tried company of the Land Commissioners.

The Land Commission has been in many senses unfortunate. The original German member, a gentleman of the name of Eggert, fell early into precarious health; his work was from the first interrupted, he was at last (to the regret of all that knew him) invalided home; and his successor had but just arrived. In like manner, the first American commissioner, Henry C. Ide, a man of character and intelligence, was recalled (I believe by private affairs) when he was but just settling into the spirit of the work; and though his place was promptly filled by ex-Governor Ormsbee, a worthy successor, distinguished by strong and vivacious common sense, the break was again sensible. The English commissioner, my friend Bazett Michael Haggard, is thus the only one who has continued at his post since the beginning. And yet, in spite of these unusual changes, the Commission has a record perhaps unrivalled among international commissions. It has been unanimous practically from the first until the last; and out of some four hundred cases disposed of, there is but one on which the members were divided. It was the more unfortunate they should have early fallen in a difficulty with the chief justice. The original ground of this is supposed to be a difference of opinion as to the import of the Berlin Act, on which, as a layman, it would be unbecoming if I were to offer an opinion. But it must always seem as if the chief justice had suffered himself to be irritated beyond the bounds of discretion. It must always seem as if his original attempt to deprive the commissioners of the services of a secretary and the use of a safe were even senseless; and his step in printing and posting a proclamation denying their jurisdiction were equally impolitic and undignified. The dispute had a secondary result worse than itself. The gentleman appointed to be Natives' Advocate shared the chief justice's opinion, was his close intimate, advised with him almost daily, and drifted at last into an attitude of opposition to his colleagues. He suffered himself besides (being a layman in law) to embrace the interest of his clients with something of the warmth of a partisan. Disagreeable scenes occurred in court; the advocate was more than once reproved, he was warned that his consultations with the judge of appeal tended to damage his own character and to lower the credit of the appellate court. Having lost some cases on which he set importance, it should seem that he spoke unwisely among natives. A sudden cry of colour prejudice went up; and Samoans were heard to assure each other that it was useless to appear before the Land Commission, which was sworn to support the whites.

This deplorable state of affairs was brought to an end by the departure from Samoa of the Natives' Advocate. He was succeeded pro tempore by a young New Zealander, E. W. Gurr, not much more versed in law than himself, and very much less so in Samoan. Whether by more skill or better fortune, Gurr has been able in the course of a few weeks to recover for the natives several important tracts of land; and the prejudice against the Commission seems to be abating as fast as it arose. I should not omit to say that, in the eagerness of the original advocate, there was much that was amiable; nor must I fail to point out how much there was of blindness. Fired by the ardour of pursuit, he seems to have regarded his immediate clients as the only natives extant and the epitome and emblem of the Samoan race. Thus, in the case that was the most exclaimed against as "an injustice to natives," his client, Puaauli, was certainly nonsuited. But in that intricate affair who lost the money? The German firm. And who got the land? Other natives. To twist such a decision into evidence, either of a prejudice against Samoans or a partiality to whites, is to keep one eye shut and have the other bandaged.

And lastly, one word as to the future. Laupepa and Mataafa stand over against each other, rivals with no third competitor. They may be said to hold the great name of Malietoa in commission; each has borne the style, each exercised the authority, of a Samoan king; one is secure of the small but compact and fervent following of the Catholics, the other has the sympathies of a large part of the Protestant majority, and upon any sign of Catholic aggression would have more. With men so nearly balanced, it may be asked whether a prolonged successful exercise of power be possible for either. In the case of the feeble Laupepa, it is certainly not; we have the proof before us. Nor do I think we should judge, from what we see to-day, that it would be possible, or would continue to be possible, even for the kingly Mataafa.

It is always the easier game to be in opposition. The tale of David and Saul would infallibly be re-enacted; once more we shall have two kings in the land,—the latent and the patent; and the house of the first will become once more the resort of "every one that is in distress, and every one that is in debt, and every one that is discontented." Against such odds it is my fear that Mataafa might contend in vain; it is beyond the bounds of my imagination that Laupepa should contend at all. Foreign ships and bayonets is the cure proposed in Mulinuu. And certainly, if people at home desire that money should be thrown away and blood shed in Samoa, an effect of a kind, and for the time, may be produced. Its nature and prospective durability I will ask readers of this volume to forecast for themselves. There is one way to peace and unity: that Laupepa and Mataafa should be again conjoined on the best terms procurable. There may be other ways, although I cannot see them; but not even malevolence, not even stupidity, can deny that this is one. It seems, indeed, so obvious, and sure, and easy, that men look about with amazement and suspicion, seeking some hidden motive why it should not be adopted.

To Laupepa's opposition, as shown in the case of the Lauati scheme, no dweller in Samoa will give weight, for they know him to be as putty in the hands of his advisers. It may be right, it may be wrong, but we are many of us driven to the conclusion that the stumbling-block is Fangalii, and that the memorial of that affair shadows appropriately the house of a king who reigns in right of it. If this be all, it should not trouble us long. Germany has shown she can be generous; it now remains for her only to forget a natural but certainly ill-grounded prejudice, and allow to him, who was sole king before the plenipotentiaries assembled, and who would be sole king to-morrow if the Berlin Act could be rescinded, a fitting share of rule. The future of Samoa should lie thus in the hands of a single man, on whom the eyes of Europe are already fixed. Great concerns press on his attention; the Samoan group, in his view, is but as a grain of dust; and the country where he reigns has bled on too many august scenes of victory to remember for ever a blundering skirmish in the plantation of Vailele. It is to him—to the sovereign of the wise Stuebel and the loyal Brandeis,—that I make my appeal.

May 25, 1892.

FOOTNOTES

{1} Brother and successor of Theodor.

About Author

Childhood and youth

Stevenson was born at 8 Howard Place, Edinburgh, Scotland on 13 November 1850 to Thomas Stevenson (1818–87), a leading lighthouse engineer, and his wife Margaret Isabella (born Balfour, 1829–97). He was christened Robert Lewis Balfour Stevenson. At about age 18, he changed the spelling of "Lewis" to "Louis", and he dropped "Balfour" in 1873.

Lighthouse design was the family's profession; Thomas's father (Robert's grandfather) was civil engineer Robert Stevenson, and Thomas's brothers (Robert's uncles) Alan and David were in the same field. Thomas's maternal grandfather Thomas Smith had been in the same profession. However, Robert's mother's family were gentry, tracing their lineage back to Alexander Balfour who had held the lands of Inchyra in Fife in the fifteenth century. His mother's father Lewis Balfour (1777–1860) was a minister of the Church of Scotland at nearby Colinton, and her siblings included physician George William Balfour and marine engineer James Balfour. Stevenson spent the greater part of his boyhood holidays in his maternal grandfather's house. "Now I often wonder what I inherited from this old minister," Stevenson wrote. "I must suppose, indeed, that he was fond of preaching sermons, and so am I, though I never heard it maintained that either of us loved to hear them."

Lewis Balfour and his daughter both had weak chests, so they often needed to stay in warmer climates for their health. Stevenson inherited a tendency to coughs and fevers, exacerbated when the family moved to a damp, chilly house at 1 Inverleith Terrace in 1851. The family moved again to the sunnier 17 Heriot Row when Stevenson was six years old, but the tendency to extreme sickness in winter remained with him until he was 11. Illness was a recurrent feature of his adult life and left him extraordinarily thin. Contemporaneous views were that he had tuberculosis, but more recent views are that it was bronchiectasis or even sarcoidosis.

Stevenson's parents were both devout Presbyterians, but the household was not strict in its adherence to Calvinist principles. His nurse Alison Cunningham (known as Cummy) was more fervently religious. Her mix of Calvinism and folk beliefs were an early source of nightmares for the child, and he showed a precocious concern for religion. But she also cared for him tenderly in illness, reading to him from John Bunyan and the Bible as he lay sick in bed and telling tales of the Covenanters. Stevenson recalled this time of sickness in "The Land of Counterpane" in A Child's Garden of Verses (1885), dedicating the book to his nurse.

Stevenson was an only child, both strange-looking and eccentric, and he found it hard to fit in when he was sent to a nearby school at age 6, a problem repeated at age 11 when he went on to the Edinburgh Academy; but he mixed well in lively games with his cousins in summer holidays at Colinton. His frequent illnesses often kept him away from his first school, so he was taught for long stretches by private tutors. He was a late reader, learning at age 7 or 8, but even before this he dictated stories to his mother and nurse, and he compulsively wrote stories throughout his childhood. His father was proud of this interest; he had also written stories in his spare time until his own father found them and told him to "give up such nonsense and mind your business." He paid for the printing of Robert's first publication at 16, entitled The Pentland Rising: A Page of History, 1666. It was an account of the Covenanters' rebellion which was published in 1866, the 200th anniversary of the event.

Education

In September 1857, Stevenson went to Mr Henderson's School in India Street, Edinburgh, but because of poor health stayed only a few weeks and did not return until October 1859. During his many absences he was taught by private tutors. In October 1861, he went to Edinburgh Academy, an independent school for boys, and stayed there sporadically for about fifteen months. In the autumn of 1863, he spent one term at an English boarding school at Spring Grove in Isleworth in Middlesex (now an urban area of West London). In October 1864, following an improvement to his health, he was sent to Robert Thomson's private school in Frederick Street, Edinburgh, where he remained until he went to university. In November 1867, Stevenson entered the University of Edinburgh to study engineering. He showed from the start no enthusiasm for his studies and devoted much energy to avoiding lectures. This time was more important for the friendships he made with other students in the Speculative Society (an exclusive debating club), particularly with Charles Baxter, who would become Stevenson's financial agent, and with a professor, Fleeming Jenkin, whose house staged amateur drama in which Stevenson took part, and whose biography he would later write. Perhaps most important at this point in his life was a cousin, Robert Alan Mowbray Stevenson (known as "Bob"), a lively and light-hearted young man who, instead of the family profession, had chosen to study art. Each year during vacations, Stevenson travelled to inspect the family's engineering works—to Anstruther and Wick in 1868, with his father on his official tour of Orkney and Shetland islands lighthouses in 1869, and for three weeks to the island of Erraid in 1870. He enjoyed the travels more for the material they gave for his writing than for any engineering interest. The voyage with his father pleased him because a similar journey of Walter Scott with Robert Stevenson had provided the inspiration for Scott's 1822 novel The Pirate. In April 1871, Stevenson notified his father of his decision to pursue a life of letters. Though the elder Stevenson was naturally disappointed, the surprise cannot have been great, and Stevenson's mother reported that he was "wonderfully resigned" to his son's choice. To provide some security, it was agreed that Stevenson should read Law (again at Edinburgh University) and be called to the Scottish bar. In his 1887 poetry collection Underwoods, Stevenson muses on his having turned from the family profession:

> *Say not of me that weakly I declined*
> *The labours of my sires, and fled the sea,*
> *The towers we founded and the lamps we lit,*
> *To play at home with paper like a child.*
> *But rather say: In the afternoon of time*

A strenuous family dusted from its hands

The sand of granite, and beholding far

Along the sounding coast its pyramids

And tall memorials catch the dying sun,

Smiled well content, and to this childish task

Around the fire addressed its evening hours.

In other respects too, Stevenson was moving away from his upbringing. His dress became more Bohemian; he already wore his hair long, but he now took to wearing a velveteen jacket and rarely attended parties in conventional evening dress. Within the limits of a strict allowance, he visited cheap pubs and brothels. More importantly, he had come to reject Christianity and declared himself an atheist. In January 1873, his father came across the constitution of the LJR (Liberty, Justice, Reverence) Club, of which Stevenson and his cousin Bob were members, which began: "Disregard everything our parents have taught us". Questioning his son about his beliefs, he discovered the truth, leading to a long period of dissension with both parents:

What a damned curse I am to my parents! As my father said "You have rendered my whole life a failure". As my mother said "This is the heaviest affliction that has ever befallen me". O Lord, what a pleasant thing it is to have damned the happiness of (probably) the only two people who care a damn about you in the world.

Early writing and travels

Stevenson was visiting a cousin in England in late 1873 when he met two people who became very important to him: Sidney Colvin and Fanny (Frances Jane) Sitwell. Sitwell was a 34-year-old woman with a son, who was separated from her husband. She attracted the devotion of many who met her, including Colvin, who married her in 1901. Stevenson was also drawn to her, and they kept up a warm correspondence over several years in which he wavered between the role of a suitor and a son (he addressed her as "Madonna"). Colvin became Stevenson's literary adviser and was the first editor of his letters after his death. He placed Stevenson's first paid contribution in The Portfolio, an essay entitled "Roads".

Stevenson was soon active in London literary life, becoming acquainted with many of the writers of the time, including Andrew Lang, Edmund Gosse, and Leslie Stephen, the editor of the Cornhill Magazine who took an interest in Stevenson's work. Stephen took Stevenson to visit a patient at the Edinburgh Infirmary named William Ernest Henley, an energetic and talkative man with a wooden leg. Henley became a close friend and occasional literary collaborator, until a quarrel broke up the friendship in 1888, and he is often considered to be the model for Long John Silver in Treasure Island.

Stevenson was sent to Menton on the French Riviera in November 1873 to recuperate after his health failed. He returned in better health in April 1874 and settled down to his studies, but he returned to France several times after that. He made long and frequent trips to the neighborhood of the Forest of Fontainebleau, staying at Barbizon, Grez-sur-Loing, and Nemours and becoming a member of the artists' colonies there. He also traveled to Paris to visit galleries and the theatres. He qualified for the Scottish bar in July 1875, and his father added a brass plate to the Heriot Row house reading "R.L. Stevenson, Advocate". His law studies did influence his books, but he never practised law; all his energies were spent in travel and writing. One of his journeys was a canoe voyage in Belgium and France with Sir Walter Simpson, a friend from the Speculative Society, a frequent travel companion, and the author of The Art of Golf (1887). This trip was the basis of his first travel book An Inland Voyage (1878).

Marriage

The canoe voyage with Simpson brought Stevenson to Grez in September 1876 where he met Fanny Van de Grift Osbourne (1840–1914), born in Indianapolis. She had married at age 17 and moved to Nevada to rejoin husband Samuel after his participation in the American Civil War. Their children were Isobel (or "Belle"), Lloyd, and Hervey (who died in 1875). But anger over her husband's infidelities led to a number of separations. In 1875, she had taken her children to France where she and Isobel studied art.

Stevenson returned to Britain shortly after this first meeting, but Fanny apparently remained in his thoughts, and he wrote the essay "On falling in love" for the Cornhill Magazine. They met again early in 1877 and became lovers. Stevenson spent much of the following year with her and her children in France. In August 1878, she returned to San Francisco and Stevenson remained in Europe, making the walking trip that formed the basis for Travels with a Donkey in the Cévennes (1879). But he set off to join her in August 1879, against the advice of his friends and without notifying his parents. He took second-class passage on the steamship Devonia, in part to save money but also to learn how others traveled and to increase the adventure of the journey. He then traveled overland by train from New York City to California. He later wrote about the experience in The Amateur Emigrant. It was good experience for his writing, but it broke his health.

He was near death when he arrived in Monterey, California, where some local ranchers nursed him back to health. He stayed for a time at the French Hotel located at 530 Houston Street, now a museum dedicated to his memory called the "Stevenson House". While there, he often dined "on the cuff," as he said, at a nearby restaurant run by Frenchman Jules Simoneau which stood at what is now Simoneau Plaza; several years later, he sent Simoneau an inscribed copy of his novel Strange Case of Dr Jekyll and Mr Hyde (1886), writing that it would be a stranger case still if Robert Louis Stevenson ever forgot Jules Simoneau. While in Monterey, he wrote an evocative article about "the Old Pacific Capital" of Monterey.

By December 1879, Stevenson had recovered his health enough to continue to San Francisco where he struggled "all alone on forty-five cents a day, and sometimes less, with quantities of hard work and many heavy thoughts," in an effort to support himself through his writing. But by the end of the winter, his health was broken again and he found himself at death's door. Fanny was now divorced and recovered from her own illness, and she came to his bedside and nursed him to recovery. "After a while," he wrote, "my spirit got up again in a divine frenzy, and has since kicked and spurred my vile body forward with great emphasis and success." When his father heard of his condition, he cabled him money to help him through this period.

Fanny and Robert were married in May 1880, although he said that he was "a mere complication of cough and bones, much fitter for an emblem of mortality than a bridegroom." He travelled with his new wife and her son Lloyd north of San Francisco to Napa Valley and spent a summer honeymoon at an abandoned mining camp on Mount Saint Helena. He wrote about this experience in The Silverado Squatters. He met Charles Warren Stoddard, co-editor of the Overland Monthly and author of South Sea Idylls, who urged Stevenson to travel to the South Pacific, an idea which returned to him many years later. In August 1880, he sailed with Fanny and Lloyd from New York to Britain and found his parents and his friend Sidney Colvin on the wharf at Liverpool, happy to see him return home. Gradually, his wife was able to patch up differences between father and son and make herself a part of the family through her charm and wit.

Attempted settlement in Europe and the US

Stevenson searched in vain between 1880 and 1887 for a residence suitable to his health. He spent his summers at various places in Scotland and England, including Westbourne, Dorset, a residential area in Bournemouth. It was during his time in Bournemouth that he wrote the story Strange Case of Dr Jekyll and Mr Hyde, naming the character Mr. Poole after the town of Poole which is situated next to Bournemouth. In Westbourne, he named his house Skerryvore after the tallest lighthouse in Scotland, which his uncle Alan had built (1838–44). In the wintertime, Stevenson travelled to France and lived at Davos Platz and the Chalet de Solitude at Hyères, where he was very happy for a time. "I have so many things to make life sweet for me," he wrote, "it seems a pity I cannot have that other one thing—health. But though you will be angry to hear it, I believe, for myself at least, what is is best." In spite of his ill health, he produced the bulk of his best-known work during these years. Treasure Island was published under the pseudonym "Captain George North" and became his first widely popular book; he wrote it during this time, along with Kidnapped, Strange Case of Dr Jekyll and Mr Hyde (which established his wider reputation), The Black Arrow: A Tale of the Two Roses, A Child's Garden of Verses, and Underwoods. He gave a copy of Kidnapped to his friend and frequent Skerryvore visitor Henry James.

His father died in 1887 and Stevenson felt free to follow the advice of his physician to try a complete change of climate, so he headed for Colorado with his mother and family. But after landing in New York, they decided to spend the winter in the Adirondacks at a cure cottage now known as Stevenson Cottage at Saranac Lake, New York. During the intensely cold winter, Stevenson wrote some of his best essays, including Pulvis et Umbra. He also began The Master of Ballantrae and lightheartedly planned a cruise to the southern Pacific Ocean for the following summer.

Politics

Stevenson believed in Conservatism for most of his life. His cousin and biographer Sir Graham Balfour said that "he probably throughout life would, if compelled to vote, have always supported the Conservative candidate." In 1866, Stevenson voted for Benjamin Disraeli, future Conservative Prime Minister of the United Kingdom, over Thomas Carlyle for the Lord Rectorship of the University of Edinburgh. During his college years, he briefly identified himself as a "red-hot socialist". He wrote at age 26: "I look back to the time when I was a Socialist with something like regret…. Now I know that in thus turning Conservative with years, I am going through the normal cycle of change and travelling in the common orbit of men's opinions."

Journey to the Pacific

In June 1888, Stevenson chartered the yacht Casco and set sail with his family from San Francisco. The vessel "plowed her path of snow across the empty deep, far from all track of commerce, far from any hand of help." The sea air and thrill of adventure for a time restored his health, and for nearly three years he wandered the eastern and central Pacific, stopping for extended stays at the Hawaiian Islands where he became a good friend of King Kalākaua. He befriended the king's niece Princess Victoria Kaiulani, who also had Scottish heritage. He spent time at the Gilbert Islands, Tahiti, New Zealand, and the Samoan Islands. During this period, he completed The Master of Ballantrae, composed two ballads based on the legends of the islanders, and wrote The Bottle Imp. He preserved the experience of these years in his various letters and in his In the South Seas (which was published posthumously). He made a voyage in 1889 with Lloyd on the trading schooner Equator, visiting Butaritari, Mariki, Apaiang, and Abemama in the Gilbert Islands. They spent several months on Abemama with tyrant-chief Tem Binoka, whom Stevenson described in In the South Seas.

Stevenson left Sydney on the Janet Nicoll in April 1890 for his third and final voyage among the South Seas islands. He intended to produce another book of travel writing to follow his earlier book In the South Seas, but it was his wife who eventually published her journal of their third voyage. (Fanny misnames the ship in her account The Cruise of the Janet Nichol.) A fellow passenger was Jack Buckland, whose stories of life as an island trader became the inspiration for the character of Tommy Hadden in The Wrecker (1892), which Stevenson and Lloyd Osbourne wrote together. Buckland visited the Stevensons at Vailima in 1894.

Last years

In 1890, Stevenson purchased a tract of about 400 acres (1.6 km²) in Upolu, an island in Samoa where he established himself on his estate in the village of Vailima after two aborted attempts to visit Scotland. He took the native name Tusitala (Samoan for "Teller of Tales"). His influence spread among the Samoans, who consulted him for advice, and he soon became involved in local politics. He was convinced that the European officials who had been appointed to rule the Samoans were incompetent, and he published A Footnote to History after many futile attempts to resolve the matter. This was such a stinging protest against existing conditions that it resulted in the recall of two officials, and Stevenson feared for a time that it would result in his own deportation. He wrote to Colvin, "I used to think meanly of the plumber; but how he shines beside the politician!"

He also found time to work at his writing, although he felt that "there was never any man had so many irons in the fire". He wrote The Beach of Falesa, Catriona (titled David Balfour in the US), The Ebb-Tide, and the Vailima Letters during this period.

Stevenson grew depressed and wondered if he had exhausted his creative vein, as he had been "overworked bitterly" and that the best he could write was "ditch-water". He even feared that he might again become a helpless invalid. He rebelled against this idea: "I wish to die in my boots; no more Land of Counterpane for me. To be drowned, to be shot, to be thrown from a horse — ay, to be hanged, rather than pass again through that slow dissolution." He then suddenly had a return of energy and he began work on Weir of Hermiston. "It's so good that it frightens me," he is reported to have exclaimed. He felt that this was the best work he had done.

On 3 December 1894, Stevenson was talking to his wife and straining to open a bottle of wine when he suddenly exclaimed, "What's that?", asked his wife "does my face look strange?", and collapsed. He died within a few hours, probably of a cerebral haemorrhage. He was 44 years old. The Samoans insisted on surrounding his body with a watch-guard during the night and on bearing him on their shoulders to nearby Mount Vaea, where they buried him on a spot overlooking the sea on land donated by British Acting Vice Consul Thomas Trood. Stevenson had always wanted his Requiem inscribed on his tomb:

Under the wide and starry sky,

Dig the grave and let me lie.

Glad did I live and gladly die,

And I laid me down with a will.

This be the verse you grave for me:

Here he lies where he longed to be;

Home is the sailor, home from sea,

And the hunter home from the hill.

Stevenson was loved by the Samoans, and his tombstone epigraph was translated to a Samoan song of grief. (Source: Wikipedia)